MASTERS OF SHRED GUITAR

CONTENTS

Cherry Lane Music Company
Director of Publications / Project Editor: Mark Phillips

ISBN 978-1-4768-8682-4

from Children of Bodom - *Are You Dead Yet?*

ARE YOU DEAD YET?

Music and Lyrics by
Alexi Laiho

Drop D tuning, down 1 step:
(low to high) C-G-C-F-A-D

Intro
Fast Rock ♩ = 192

N.C.

Riff A

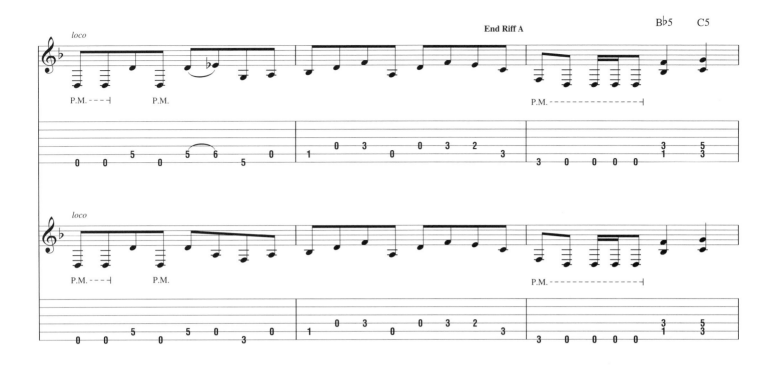

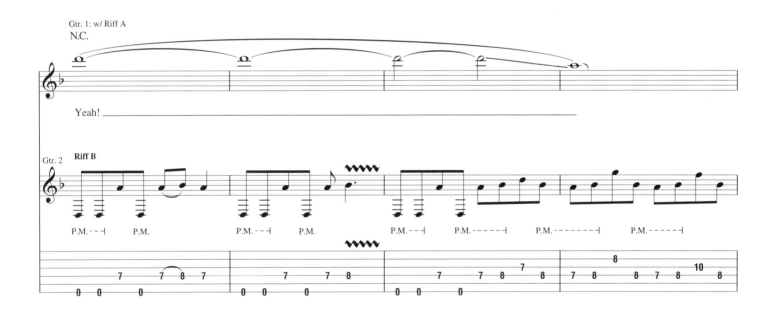

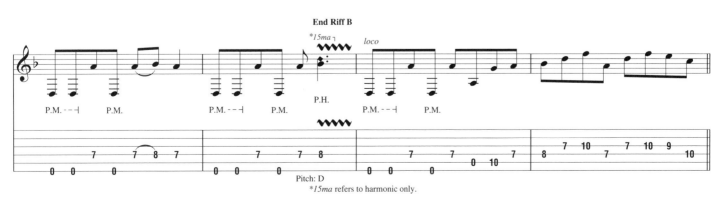

Pitch: D
*15ma refers to harmonic only.

*Chord symbol reflects combined harmony.

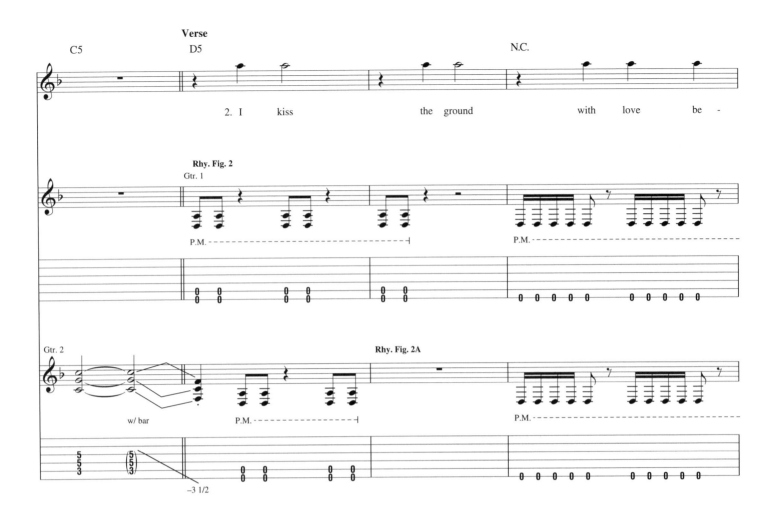

*Chord symbol reflects combined harmony.

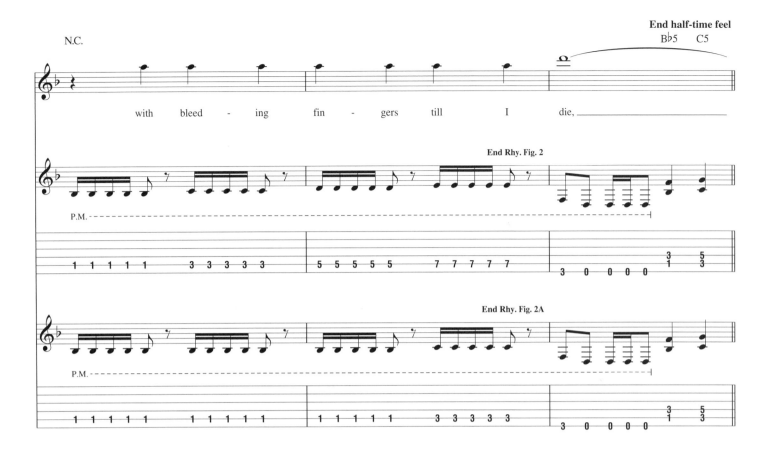

*Chord symbols reflect overall harmony.

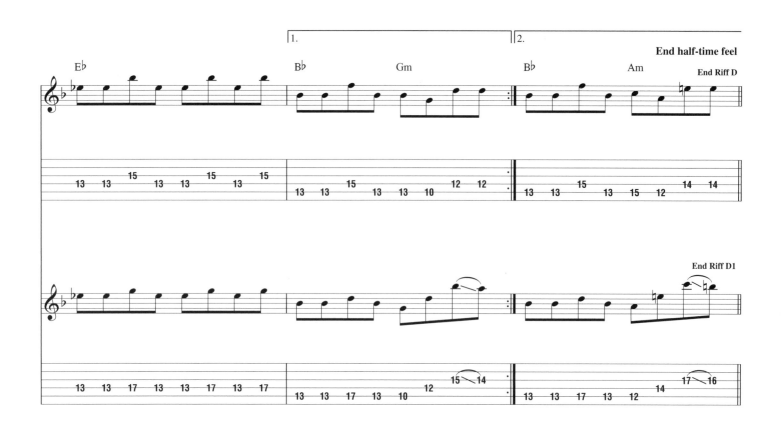

Chorus

En-e-my, take one good look at me.___ E-rad-i-cate what you will al-ways be.___

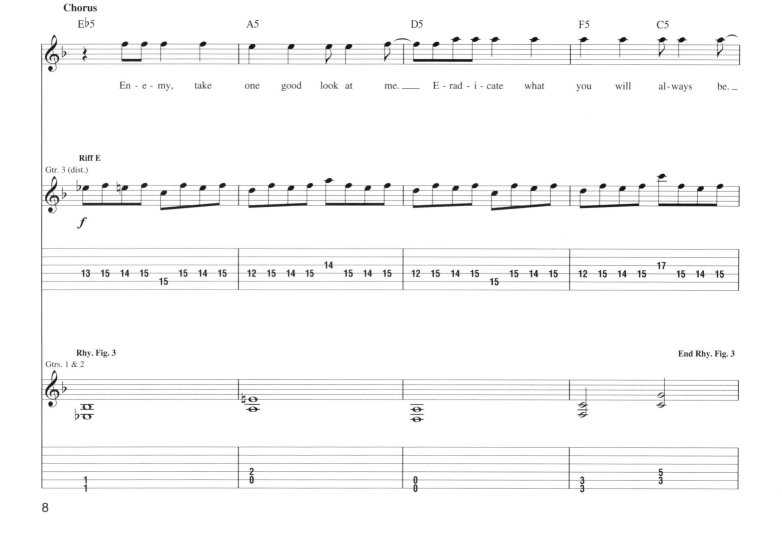

*Chord symbol reflects combined harmony.

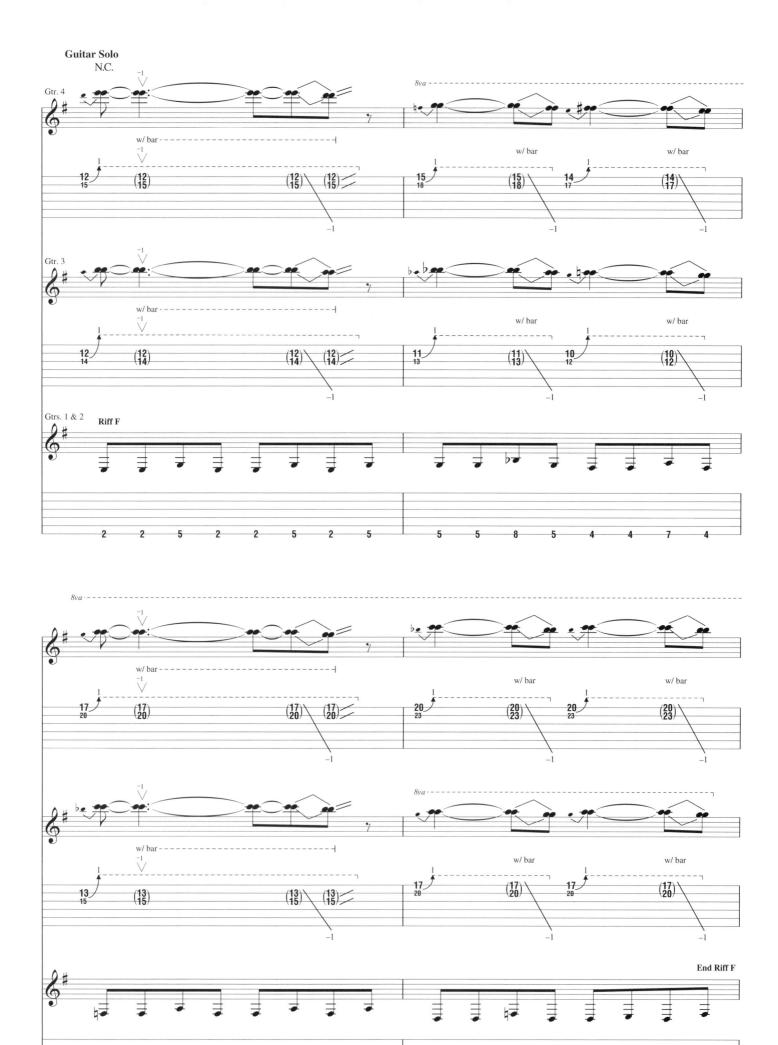

Chorus

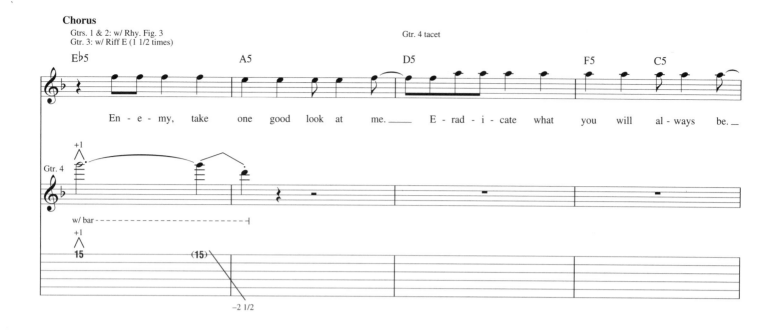

En - e - my, take one good look at me.___ E - rad - i - cate what you will al - ways be.___

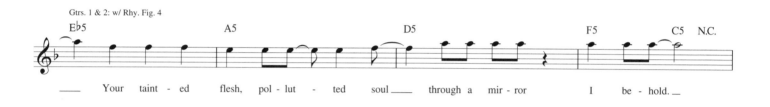

___ Your taint - ed flesh, pol - lut - ted soul___ through a mir - ror I be - hold.___

Throw a punch, shards bleed on the floor___ tear - ing me a - part,___ but I don't care an - y - more.___

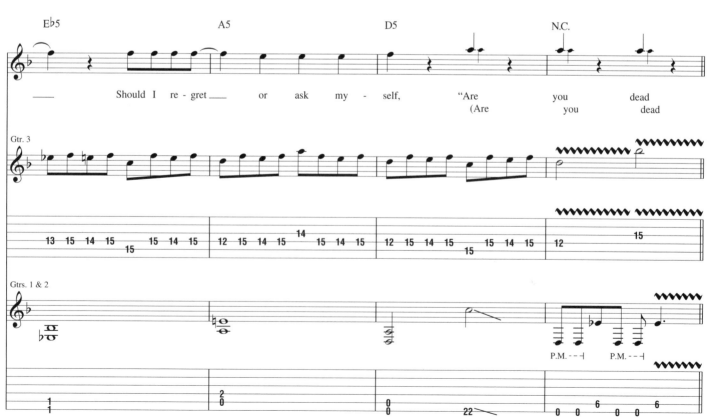

___ Should I re - gret___ or ask my - self, "Are you dead
(Are you dead

Outro
Half-time feel

15

BIRDS OF FIRE

By John McLaughlin

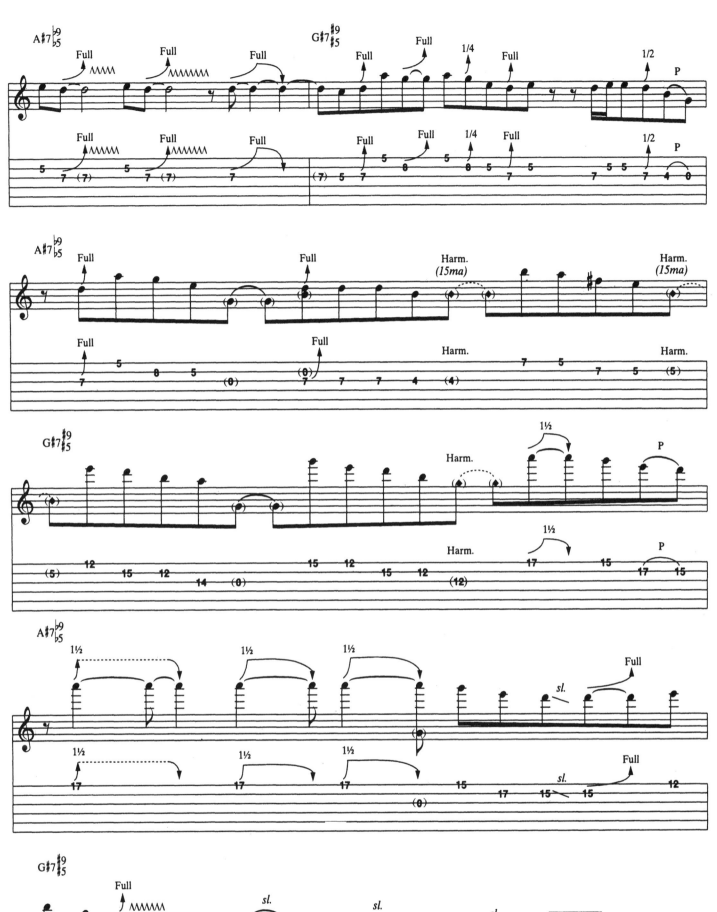
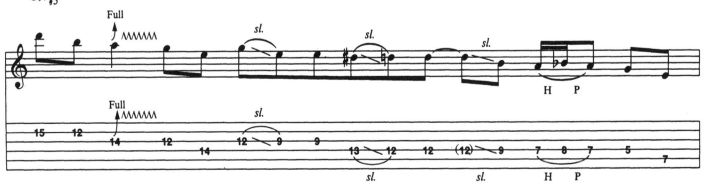

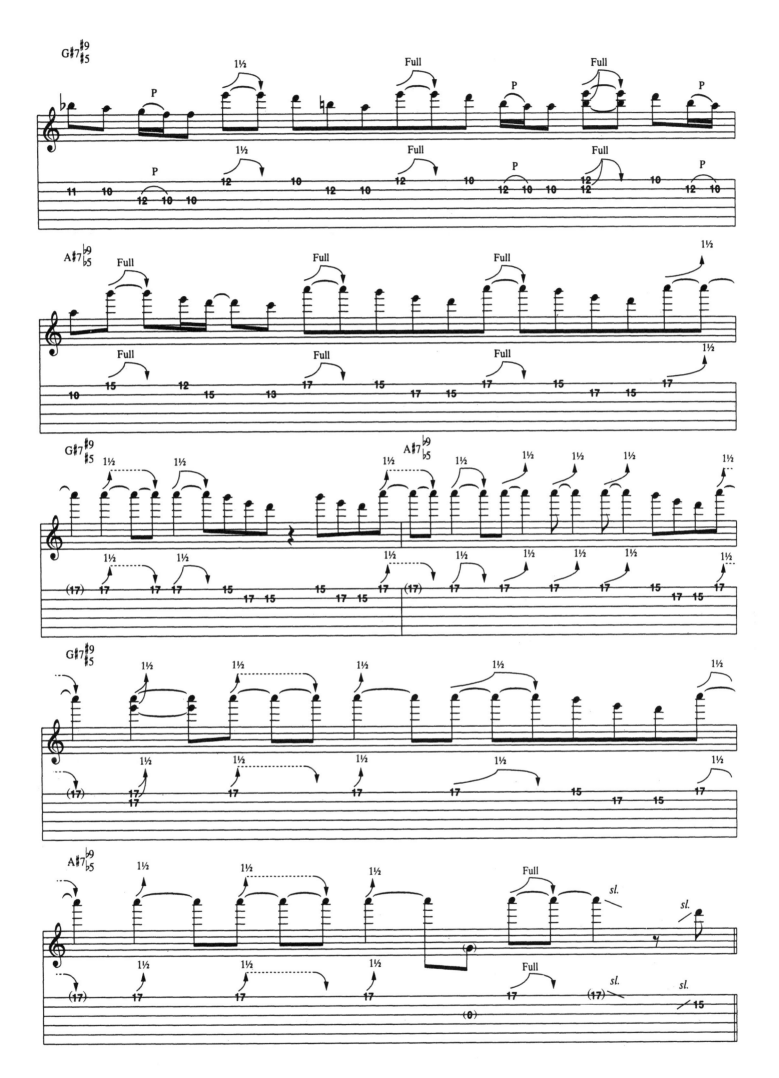

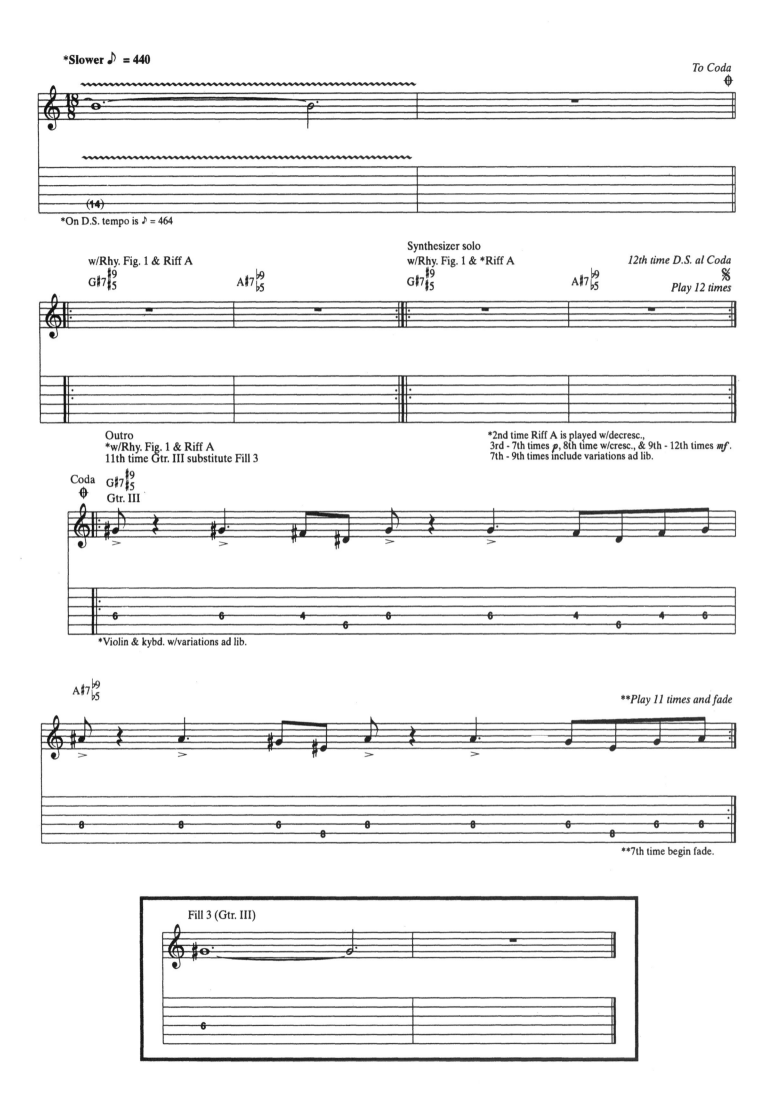

from Eric Johnson - *Ah Via Musicom*

CLIFFS OF DOVER

By Eric Johnson

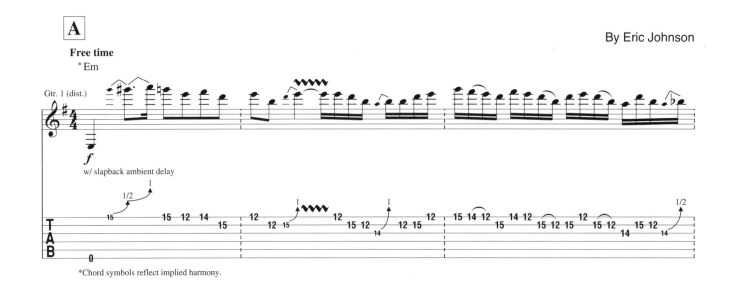

*Chord symbols reflect implied harmony.

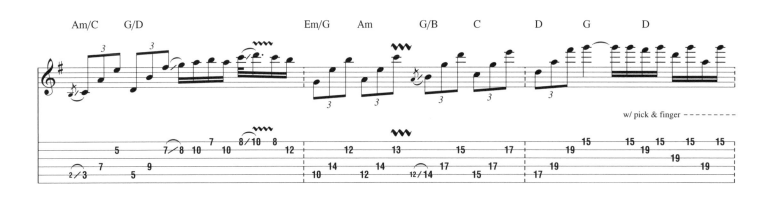

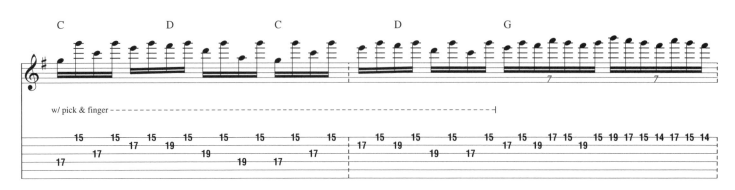

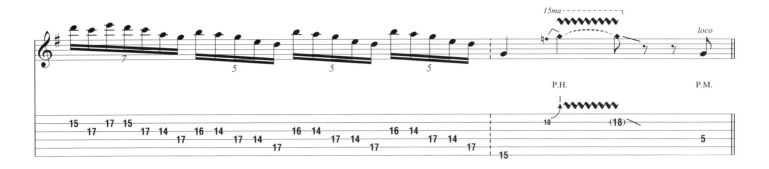

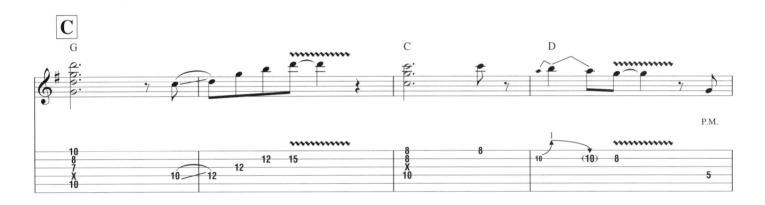

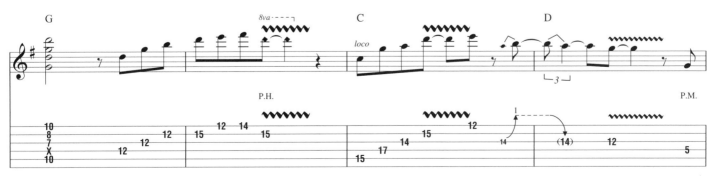

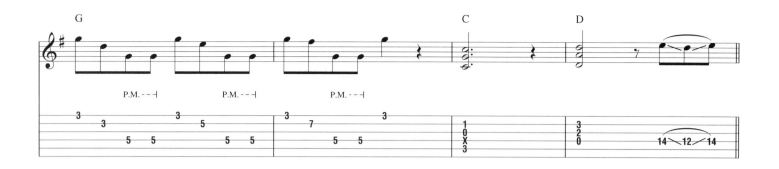

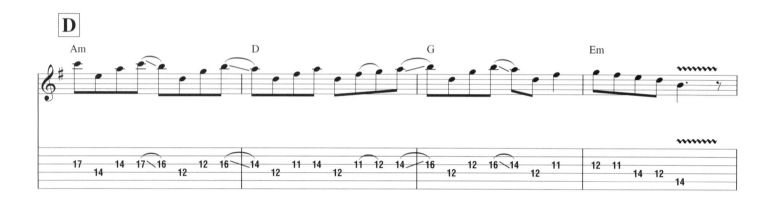

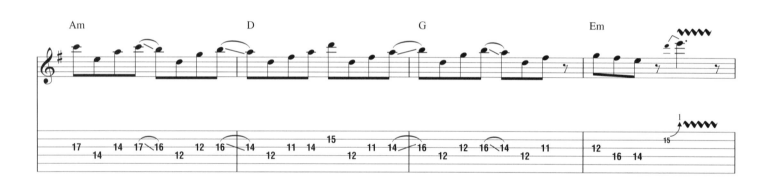

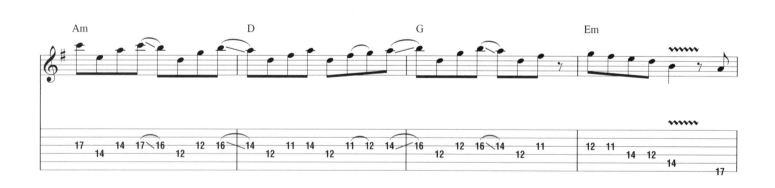

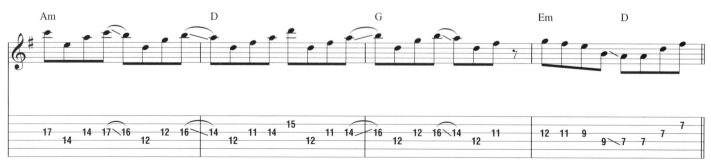

24

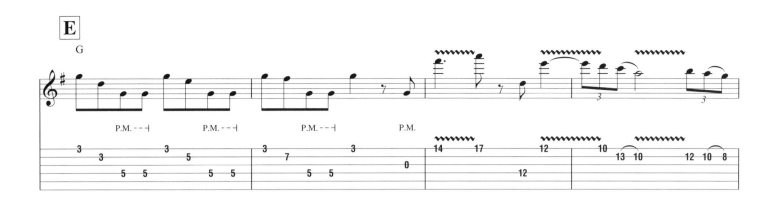

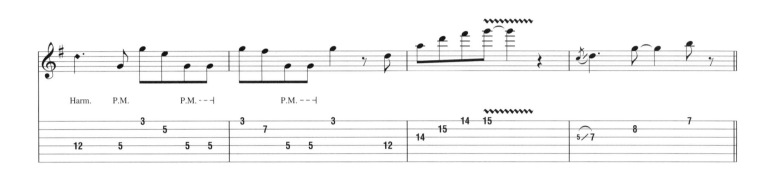

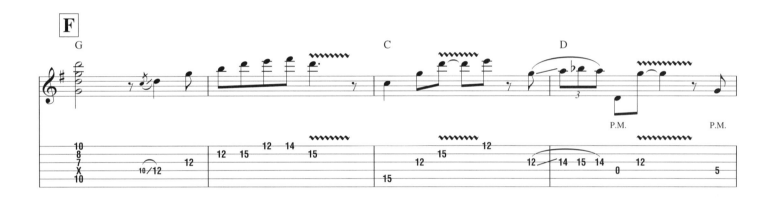

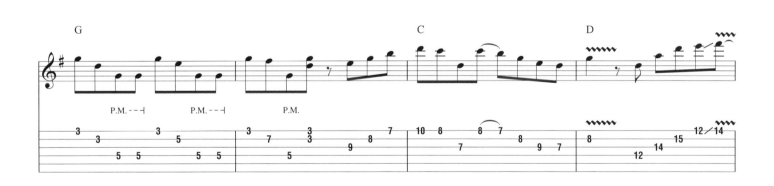

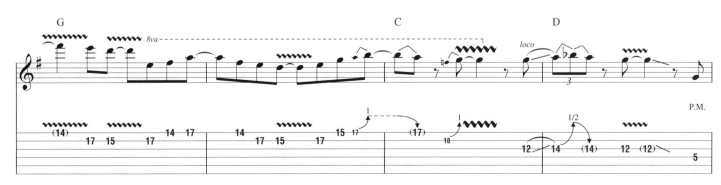

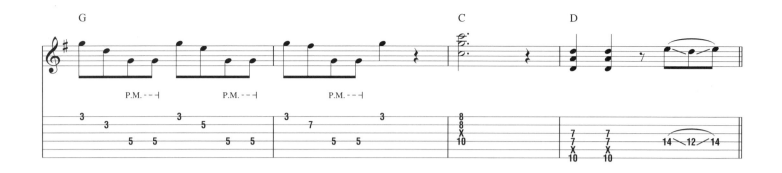

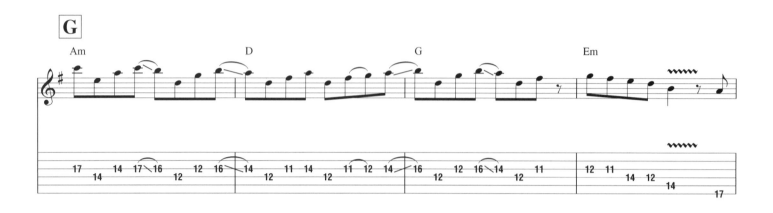

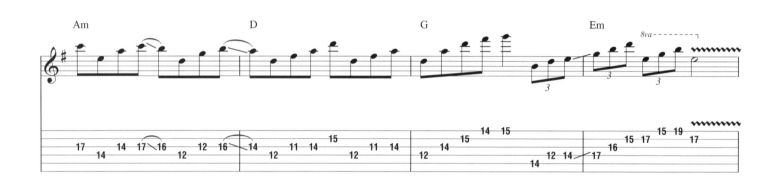

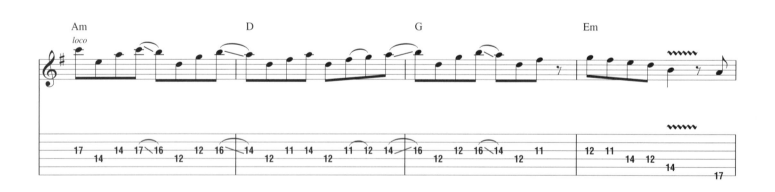

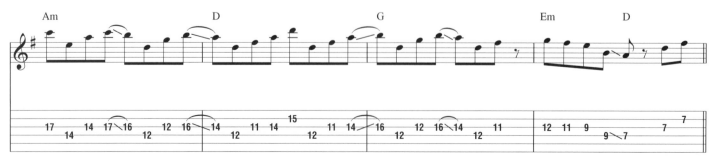

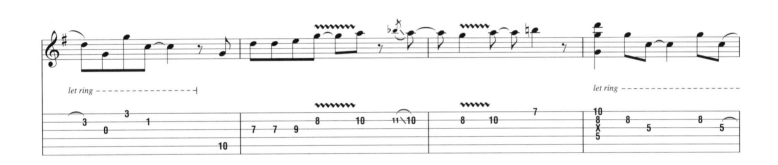

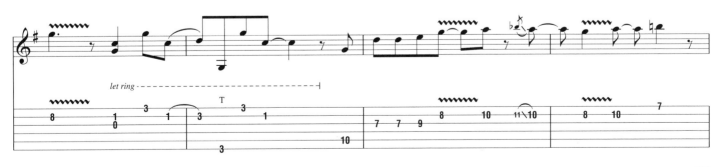

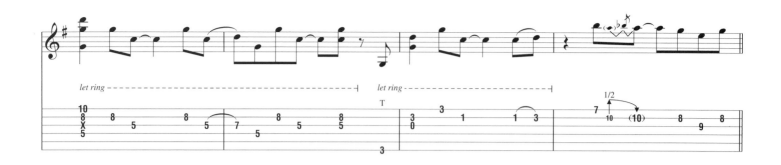

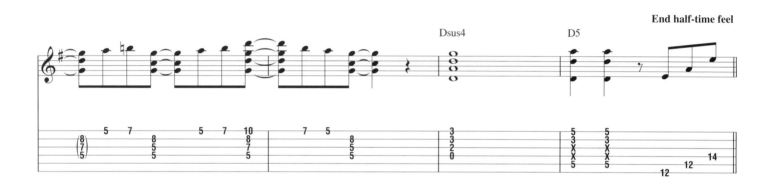

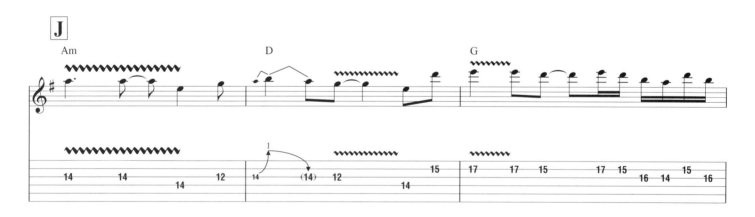

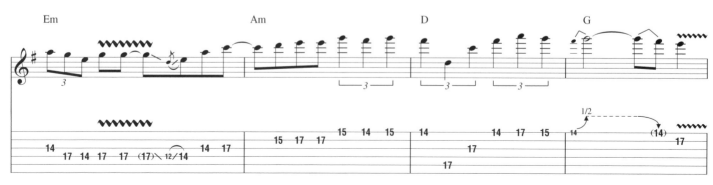

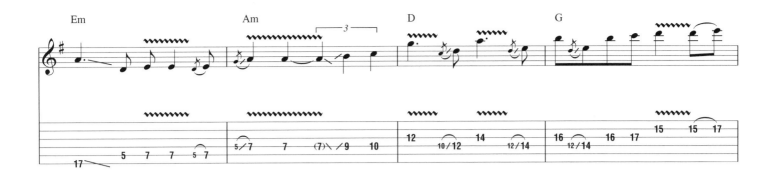

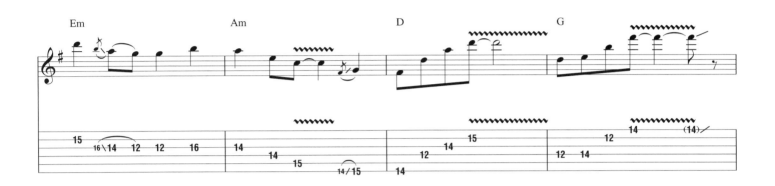

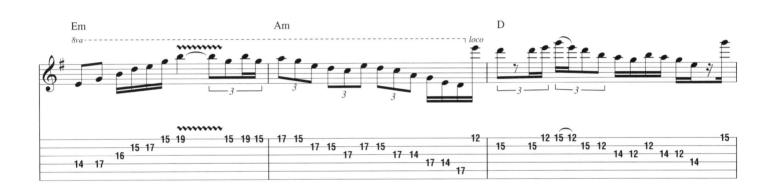

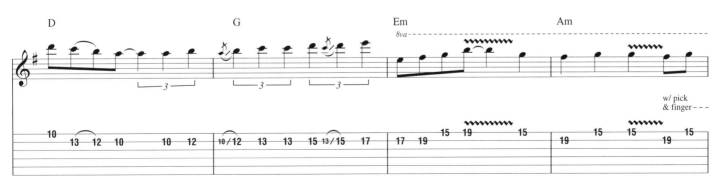

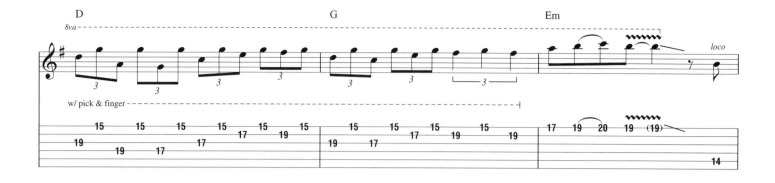

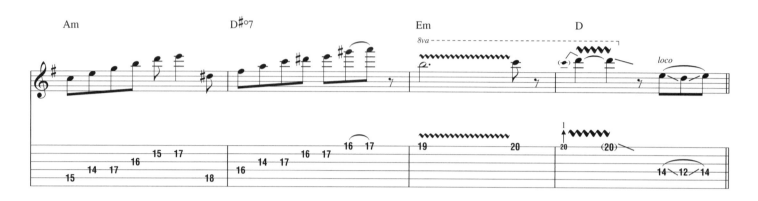

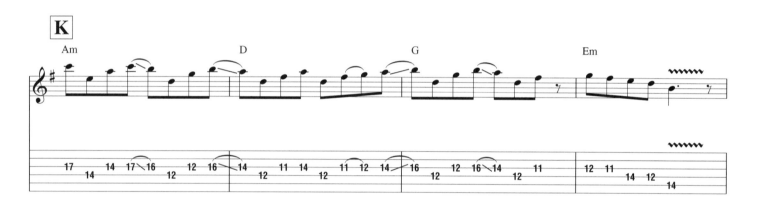

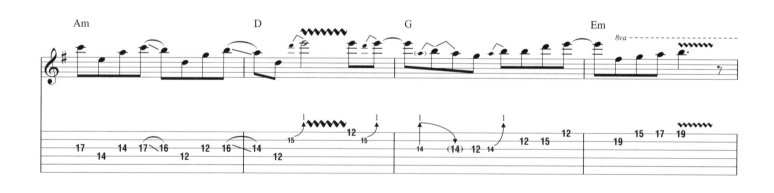

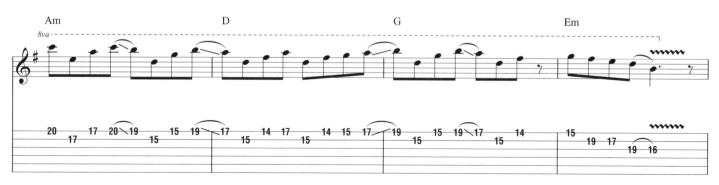

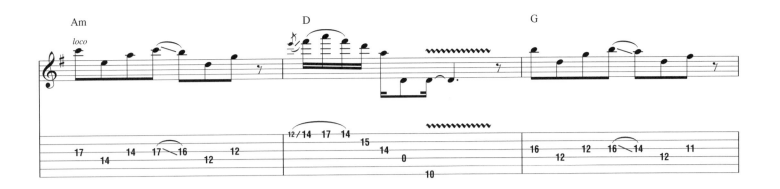

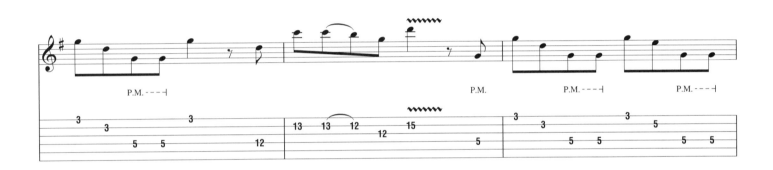

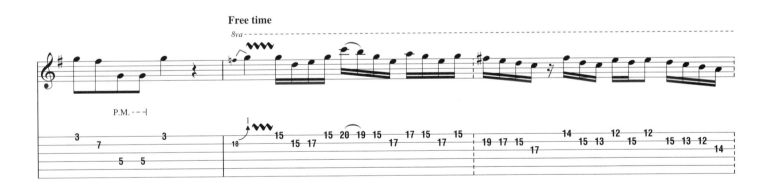

from Mr. Big - *Bump Ahead*

COLORADO BULLDOG

Words and Music by
William Sheehan, Pat Torpey,
Paul Gilbert, Eric Martin
and Tony Fanucchi

Throw a leash a-round my neck. Bot-toms up, down the hatch. It's

time to start all o-ver a-gain.

*While continuing to trem. pick, slide L.H. finger along
5th stg. towards bridge, thereby sounding harmonics.

Additional Lyrics

2. Swingin' from the rafters, losin' all control,
   Playin' a little game of cat and mouse.
   I popped the question. I've been lonely much too long.
   Last call, the drinks are on the house. *(To Pre-chorus)*

3. My sweet Lolita, a preying maneater,
   Left me in the Number Six Motel.
   How was I to know she'd strip me to the bone
   And steal away my heart as well? *(To Pre-chorus)*

from UFO - *Phenomenon*

DOCTOR, DOCTOR

Words and Music by
Phillip John Mogg and Michael Schenker

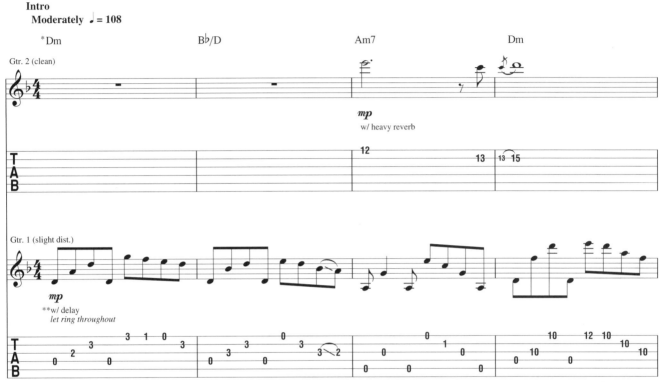

*Chord symbols reflect implied harmony.

**Set for sixteenth-note regeneration w/ 1 repeat.

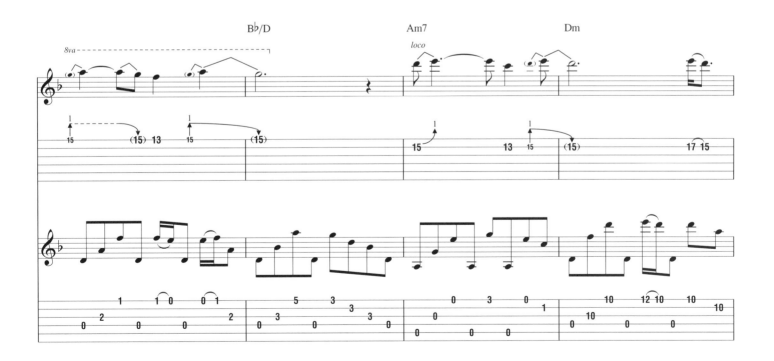

Chorus

44

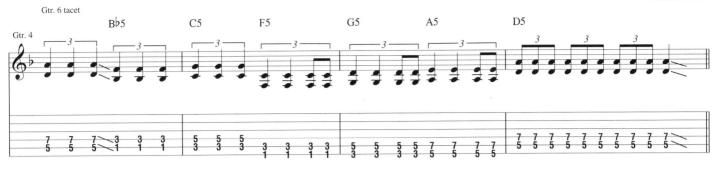

✚ **Coda**

Interlude

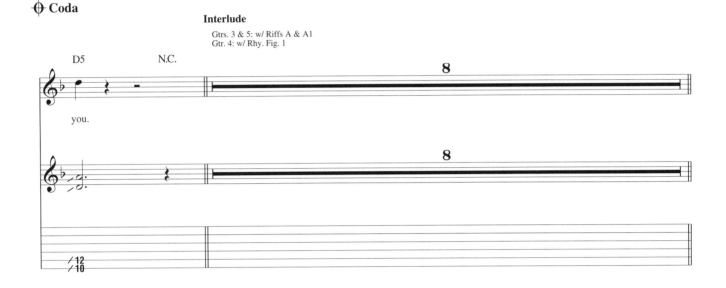

Outro

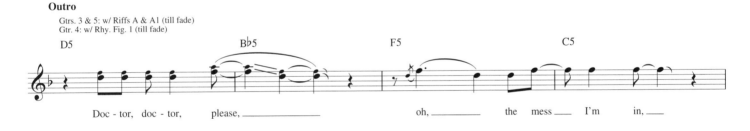

Doc - tor, doc - tor, please, _____ oh, _____ the mess ___ I'm in, ___

Begin fade

doc - tor, doc - tor, please, _____ oh, I'm go - in' fast. ___

Doc - tor, doc - tor, please, _____ oh, _____ the mess I'm in, ___

Fade out

doc-tor, doc-tor, help ___ me, help ___ me, oh, I'm go - in' mad. __ I don't...

ERUPTION

Tune down 1/2 step:
(low to high) E♭-A♭-D♭-G♭-B♭-E♭

By Edward Van Halen, Alex Van Halen,
Michael Anthony and David Lee Roth

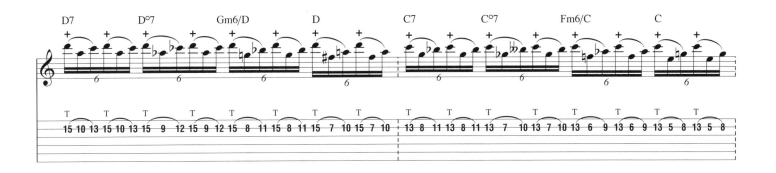

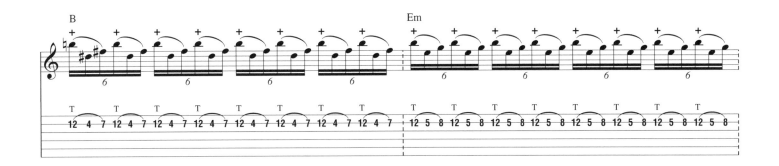

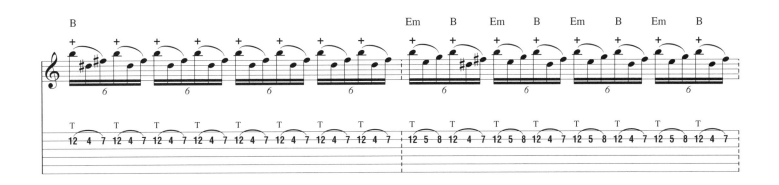

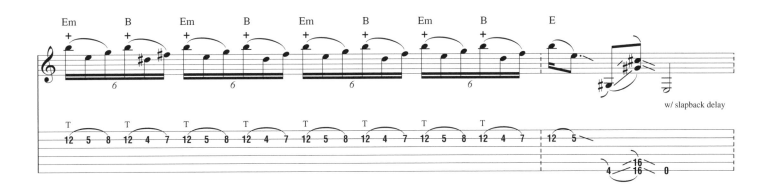

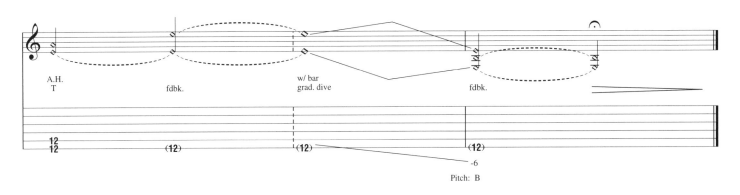

from Steve Vai - *Passion & Warfare*

FOR THE LOVE OF GOD

By Steve Vai

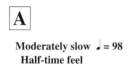

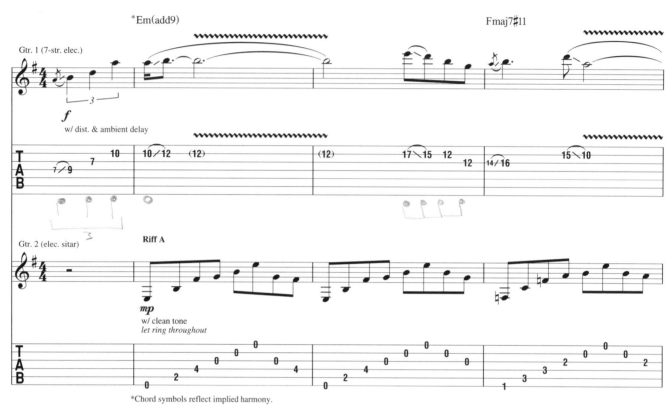

*Chord symbols reflect implied harmony.

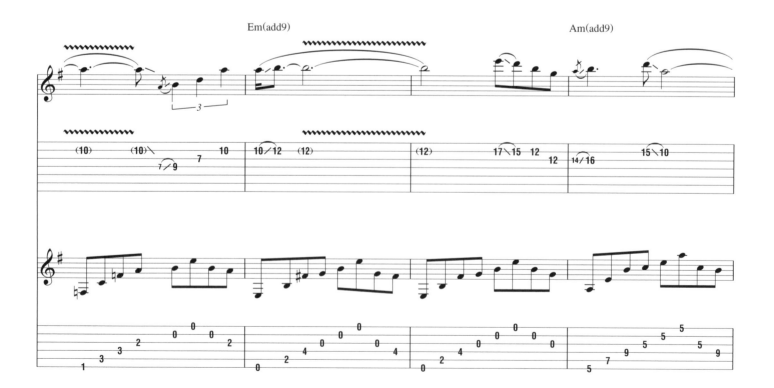

D

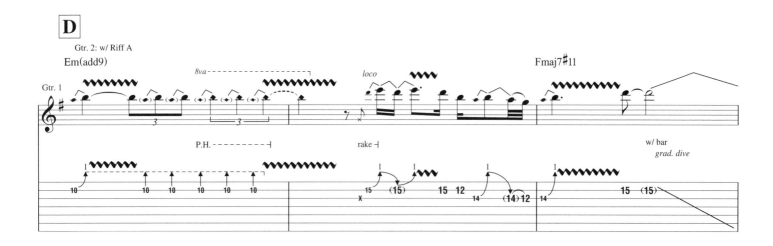

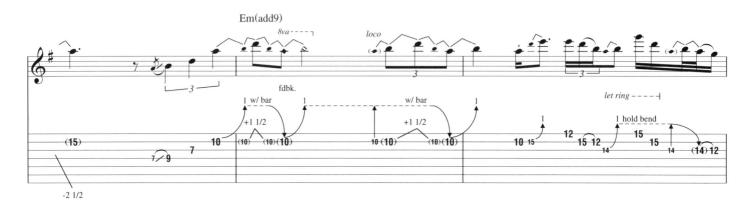

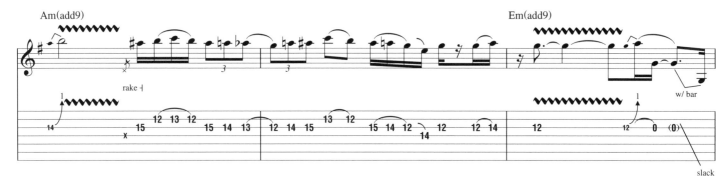

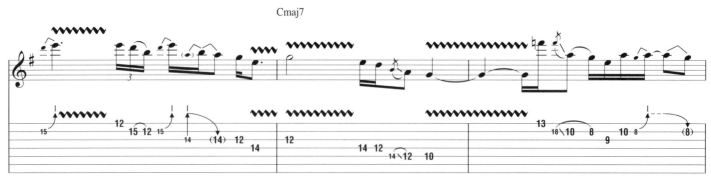

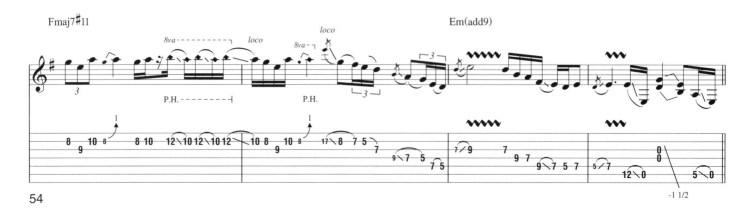

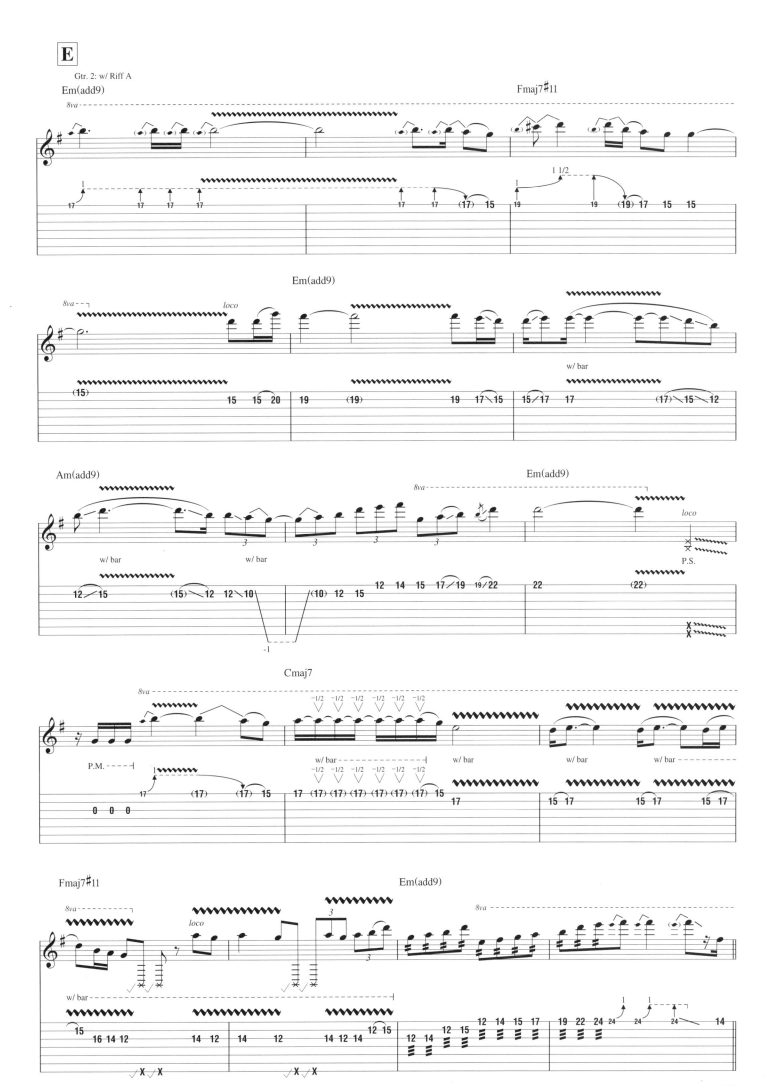

Gtr. 2: w/ Riff A

Em(add9)

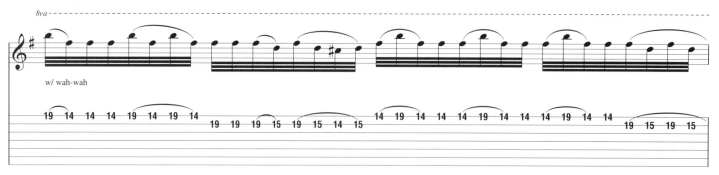

w/ wah-wah

Fmaj7#11

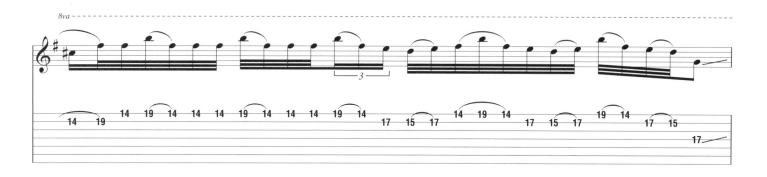

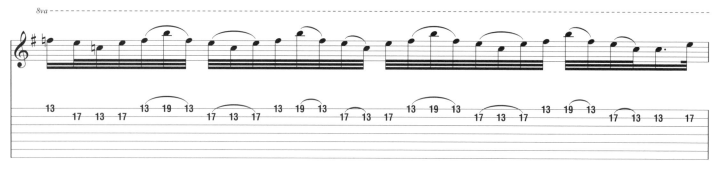

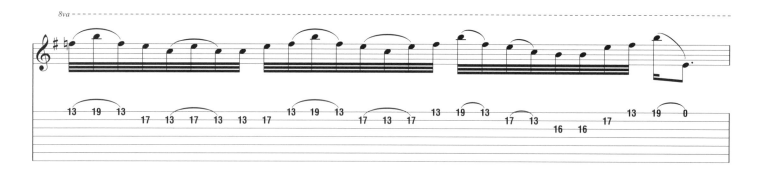

Em(add9)

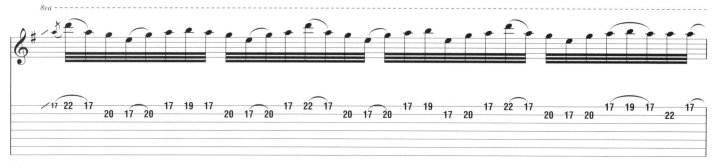

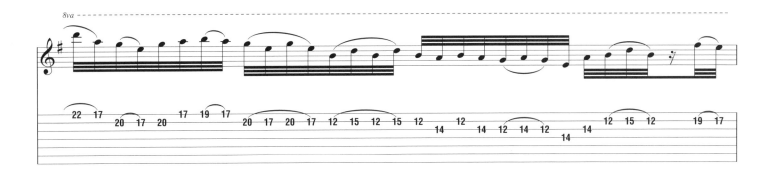

Am(add9)

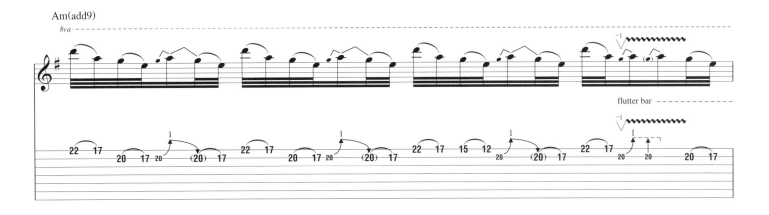

Em(add9)

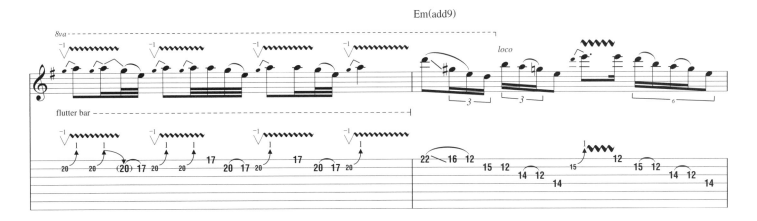

Cmaj7

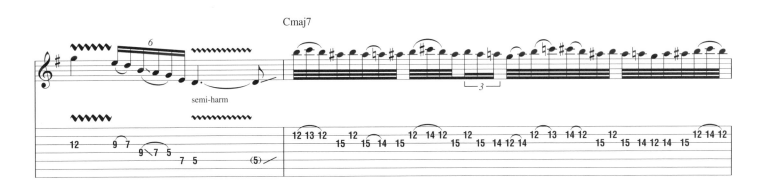

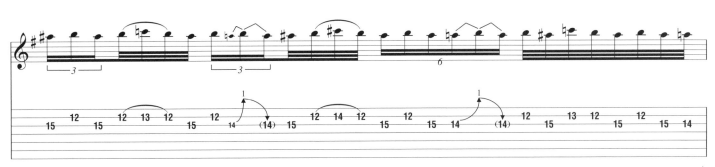

Fmaj7#11

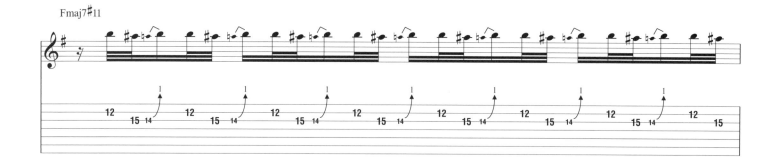

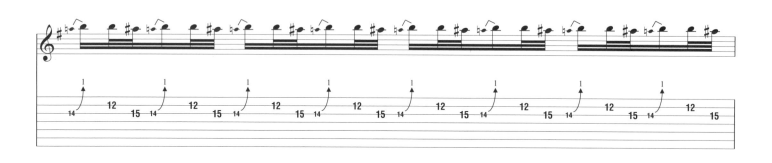

Em(add9)

G

Gtr. 2: w/ Riff B

G

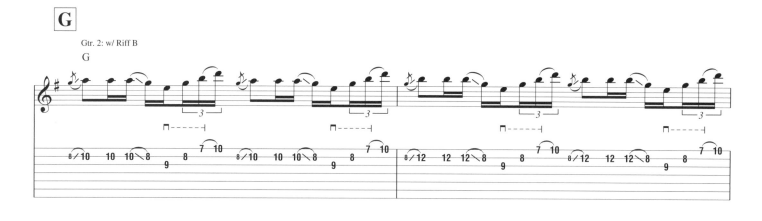

Fmaj7sus2

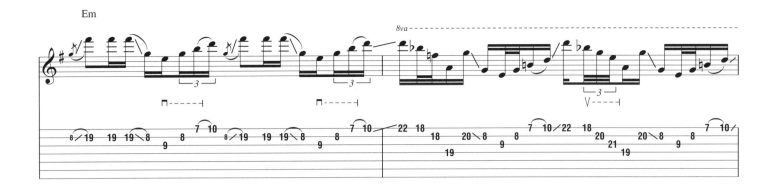

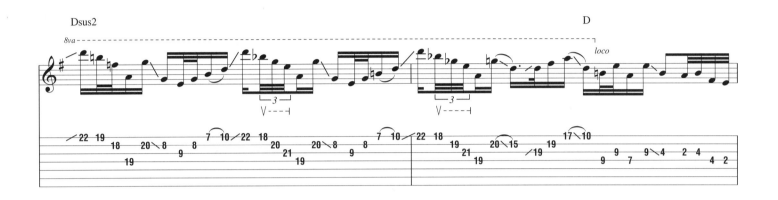

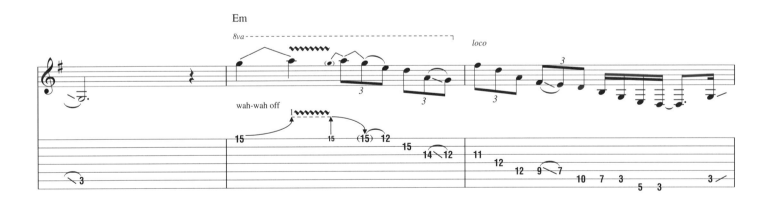

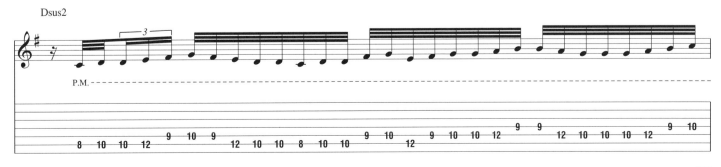

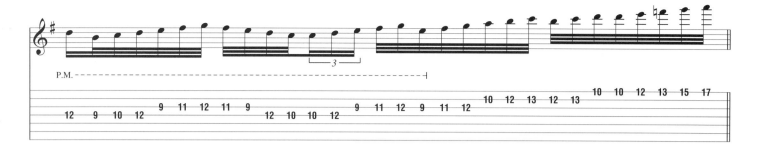

 H

Gtr. 2: w/ Riff A

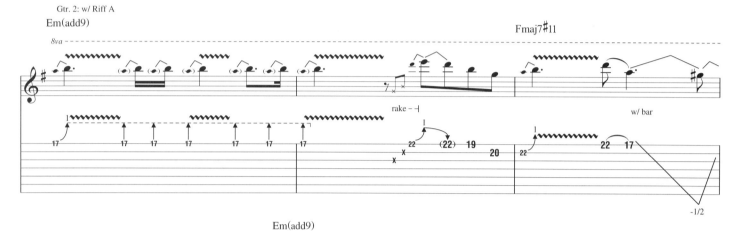

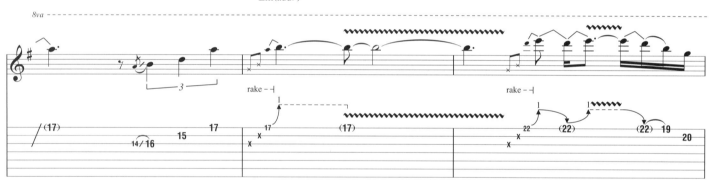

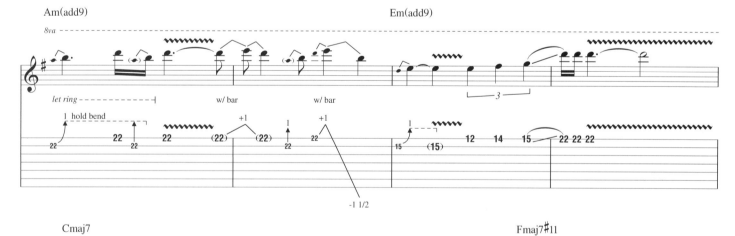

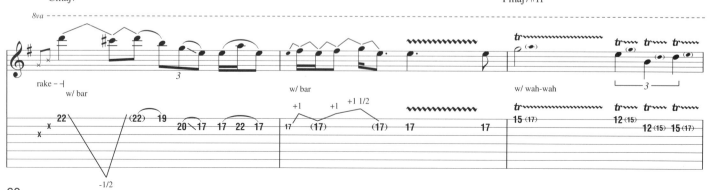

I

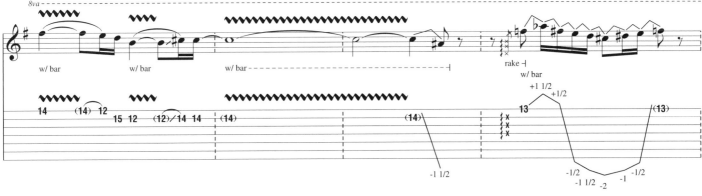

Spoken: Walking the fine line between pagan and Christian.

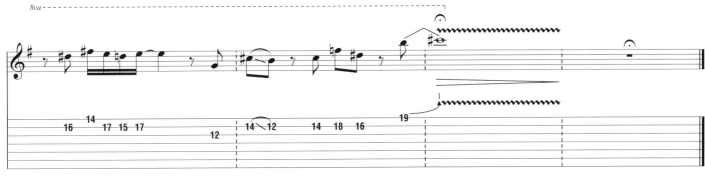

from Steve Morse - *High Tension Wires*

HIGHLAND WEDDING

Music by Steve Morse

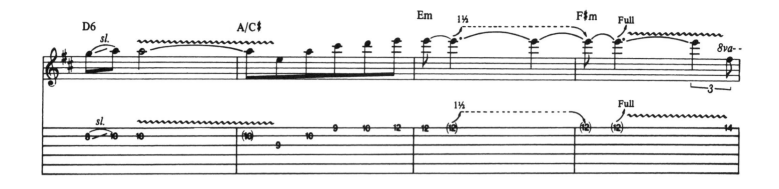

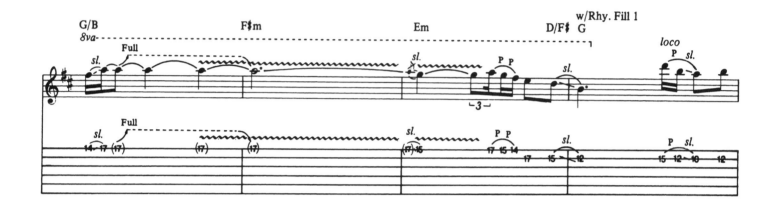

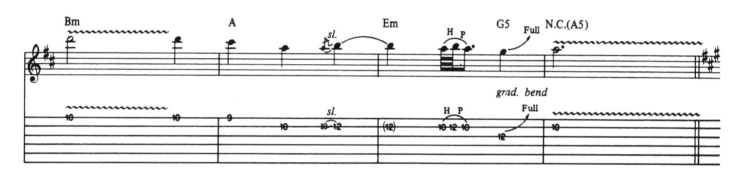

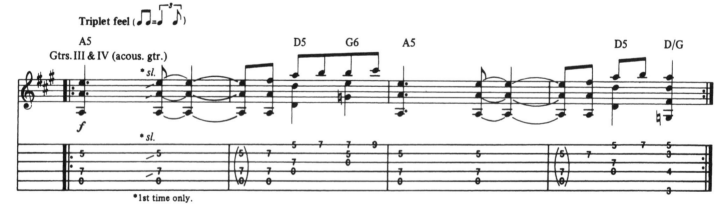

*1st time only.

Rhy. Fill 1 (Gtrs. I & II)

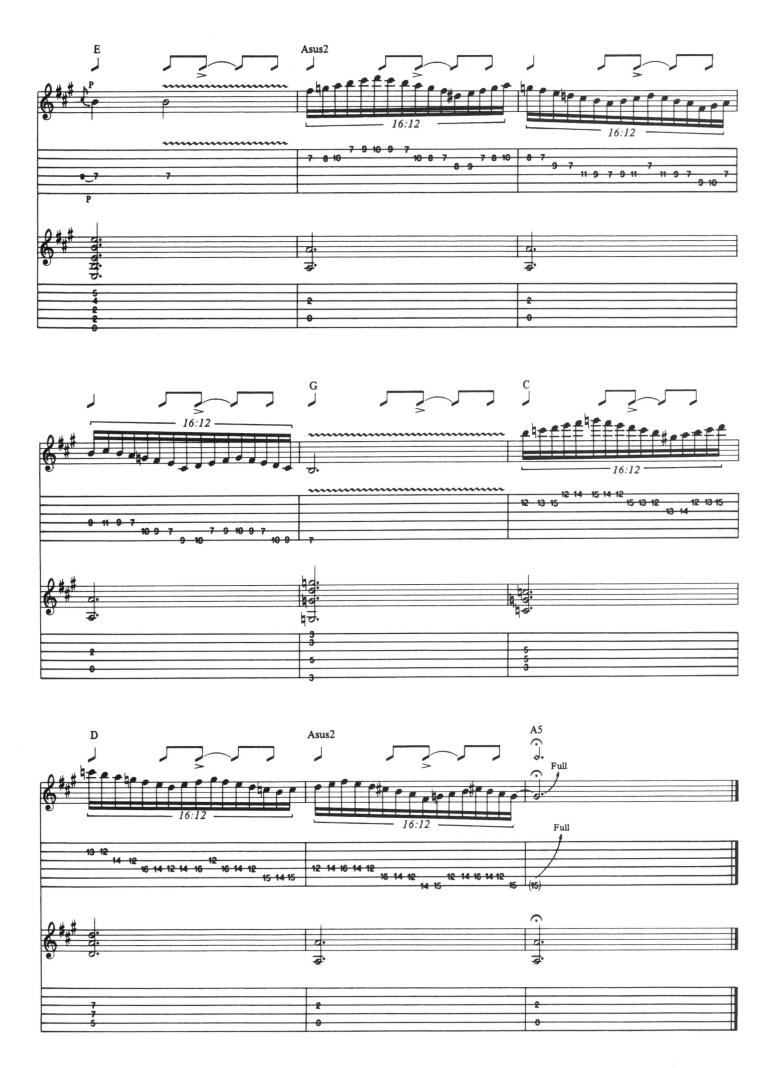

from Ozzy Osbourne - *Blizzard of Ozz*

MR. CROWLEY

Words and Music by Ozzy Osbourne,
Randy Rhoads and Bob Daisley

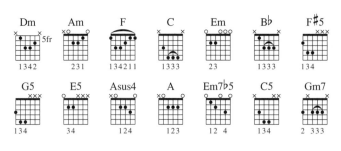

*Synth. arr. for gtr.

**See top of page for chord diagrams pertaining to rhythm slashes.

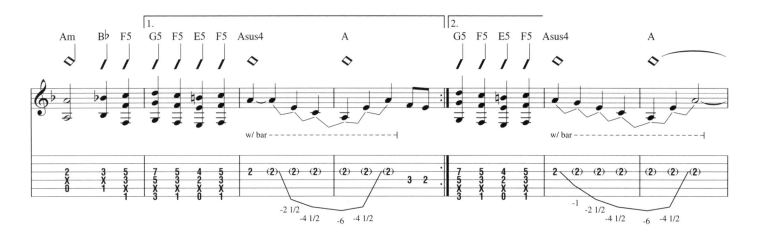

***Two gtrs. arr. for one.

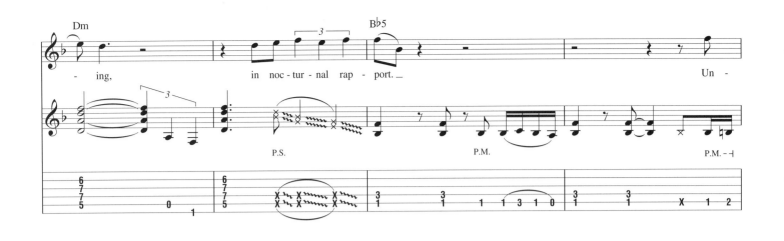

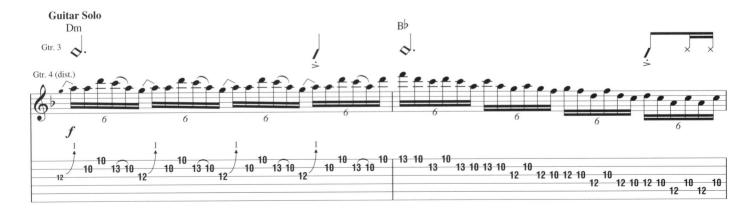

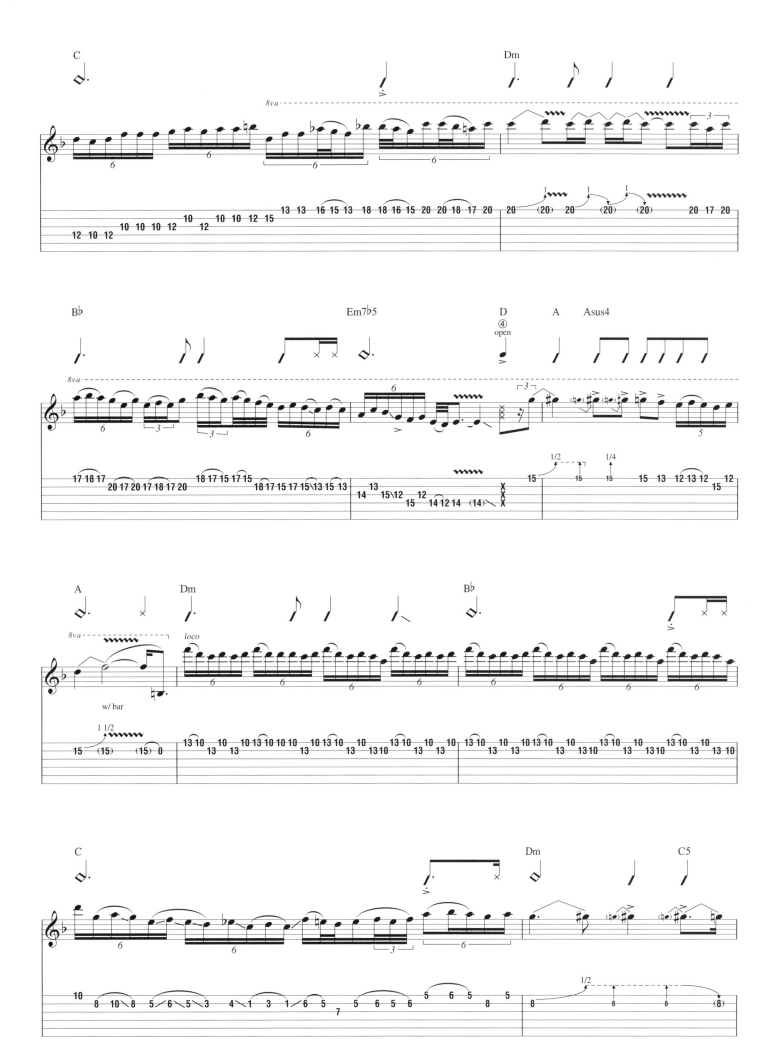

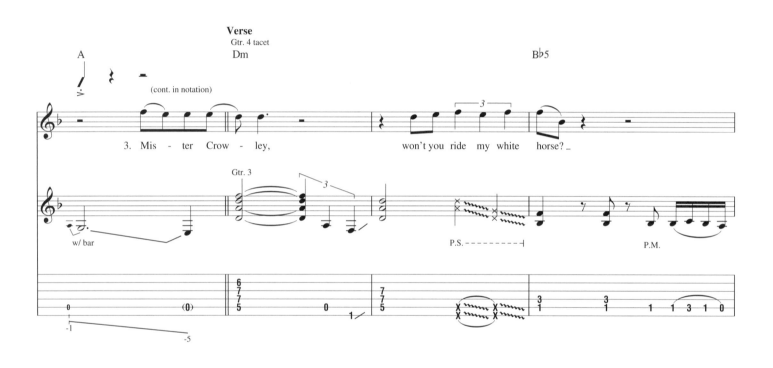

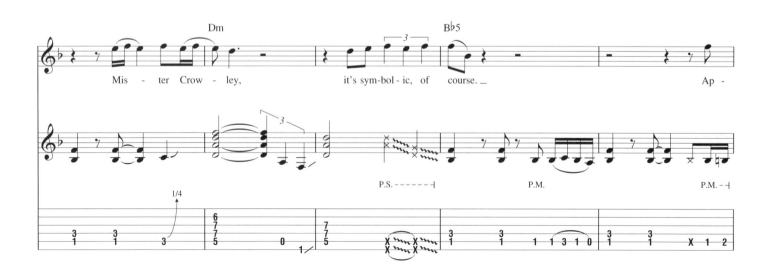

proach-ing a time that is clas - sic, I hear that maid-ens call. _____ Ap -

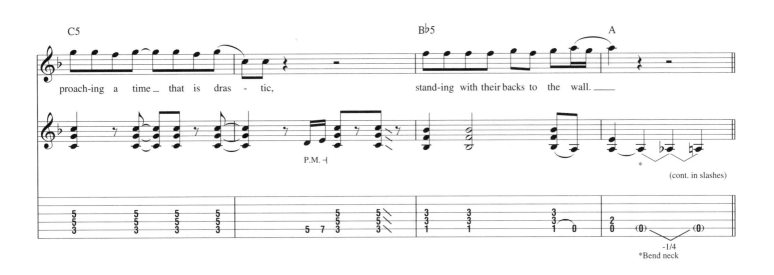

proach-ing a time that is dras - tic, stand-ing with their backs to the wall. _____

*Bend neck
-1/4

(cont. in slashes)

Interlude

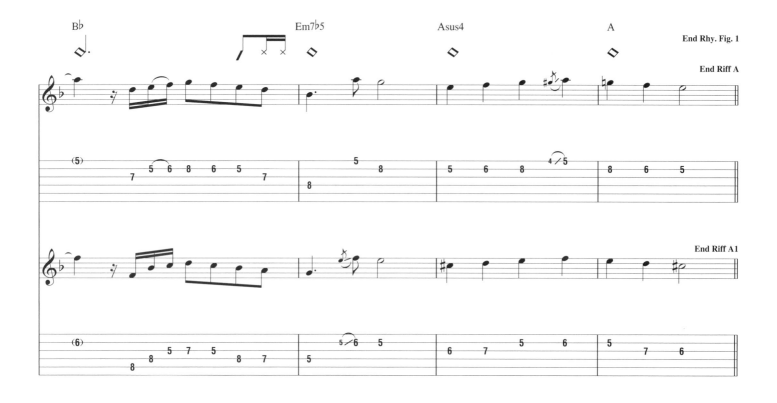

Bridge

Gtr. 3: w/ Rhy. Fig. 1
Gtrs. 4 & 5: w/ Riffs A & A1

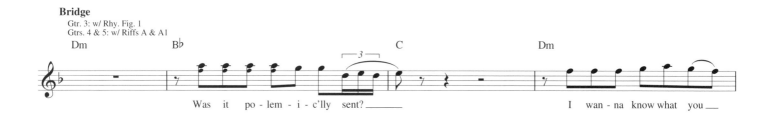

Was it po - lem - i - c'lly sent? _____ I wan - na know what you _____

meant. _____ I wan - na know, I wan - na know what you meant. _____ Yeah.

Outro - Guitar Solo

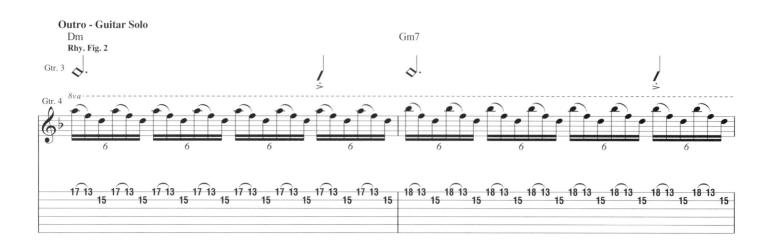

MR. SCARY

By George Lynch and Jeff Pilson

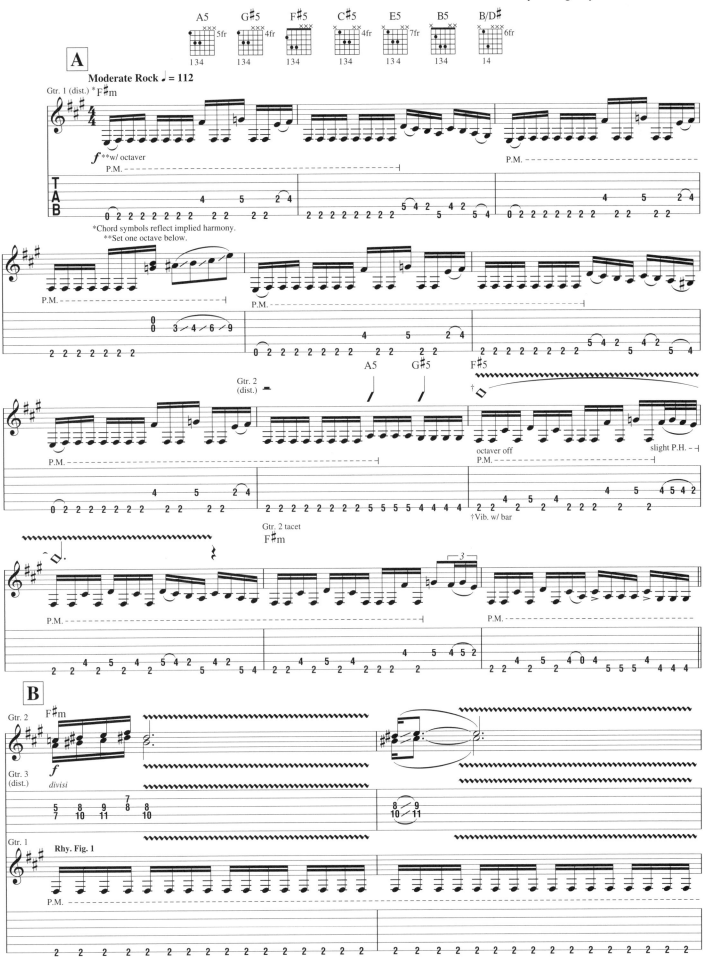

*Chord symbols reflect implied harmony.
**Set one octave below.

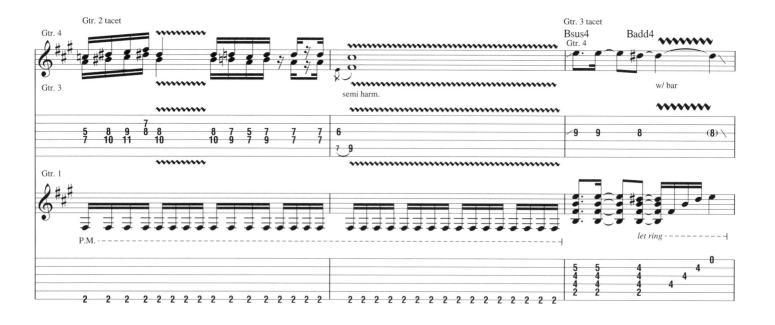

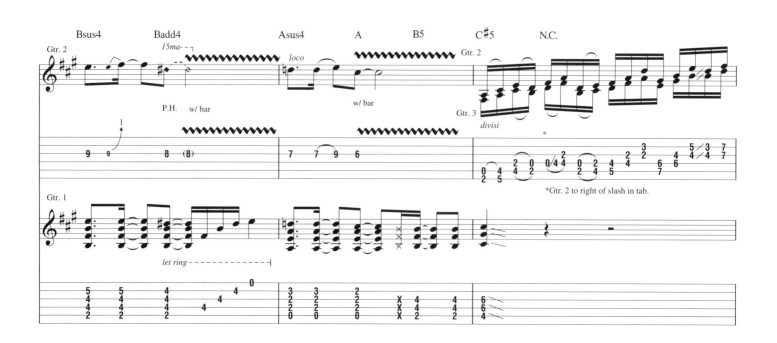

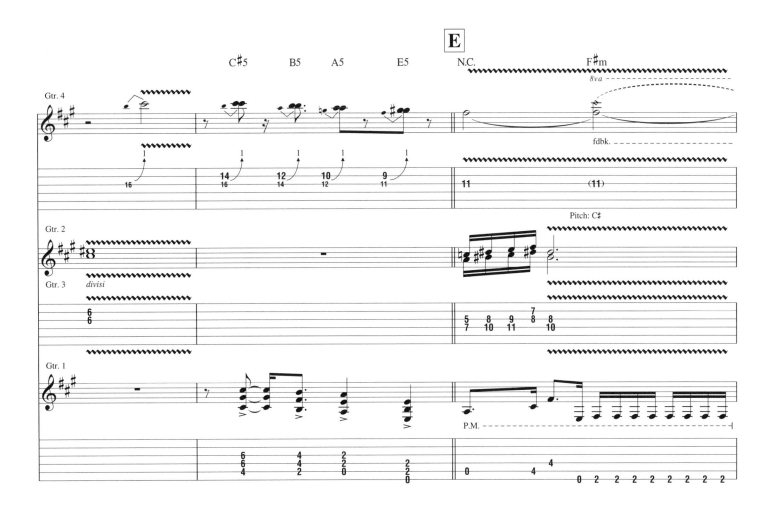

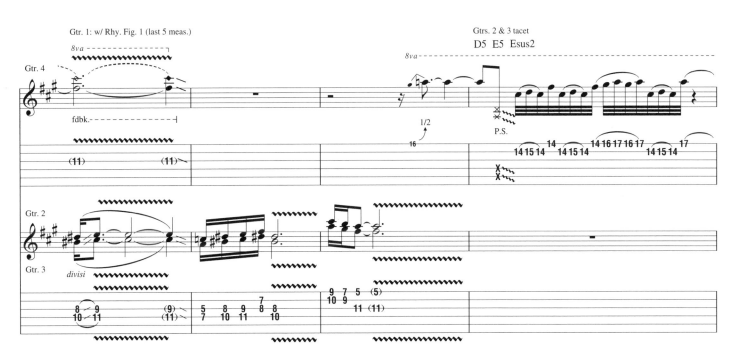

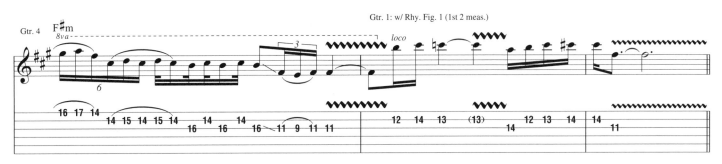

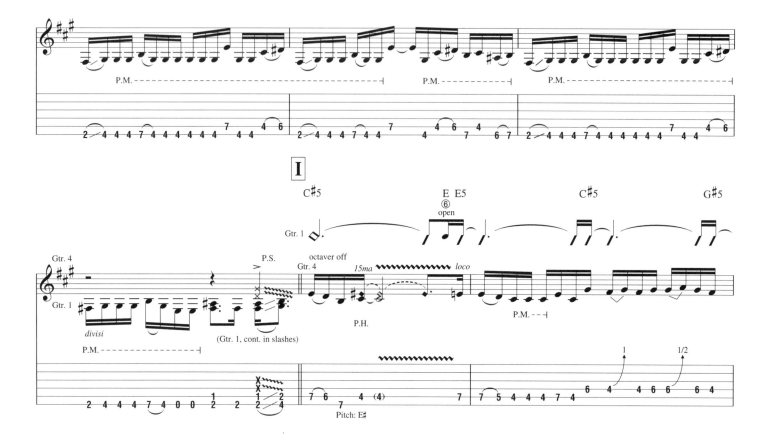

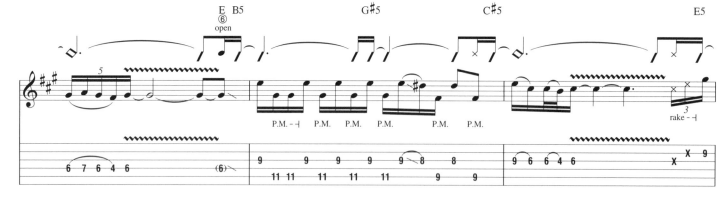

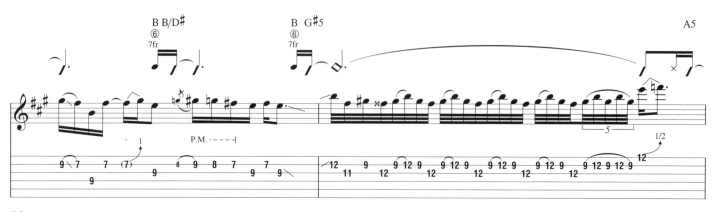

from Blues Saraceno - *Never Look Back*

NEVER LOOK BACK

Words and Music by
Blues Saraceno

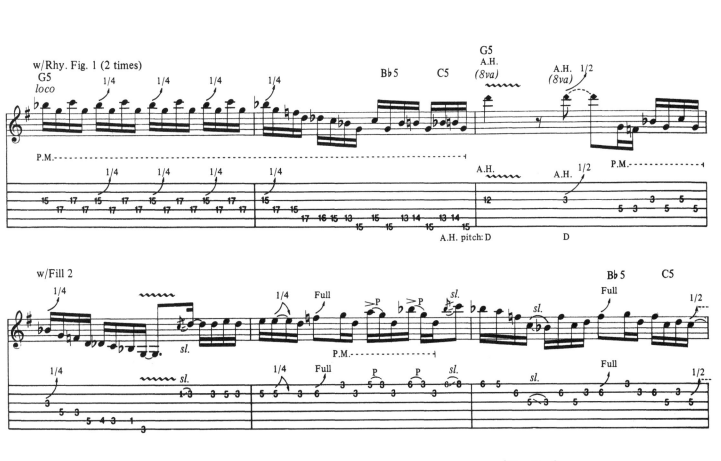

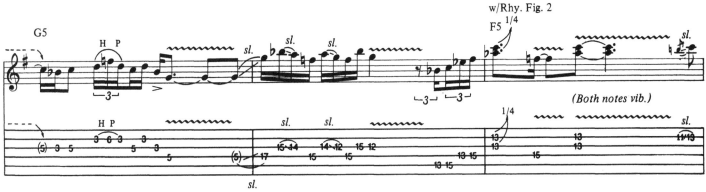

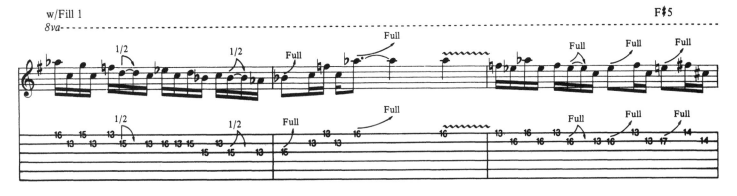

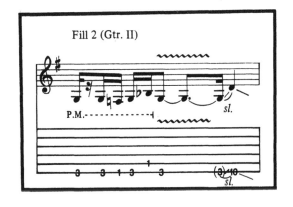

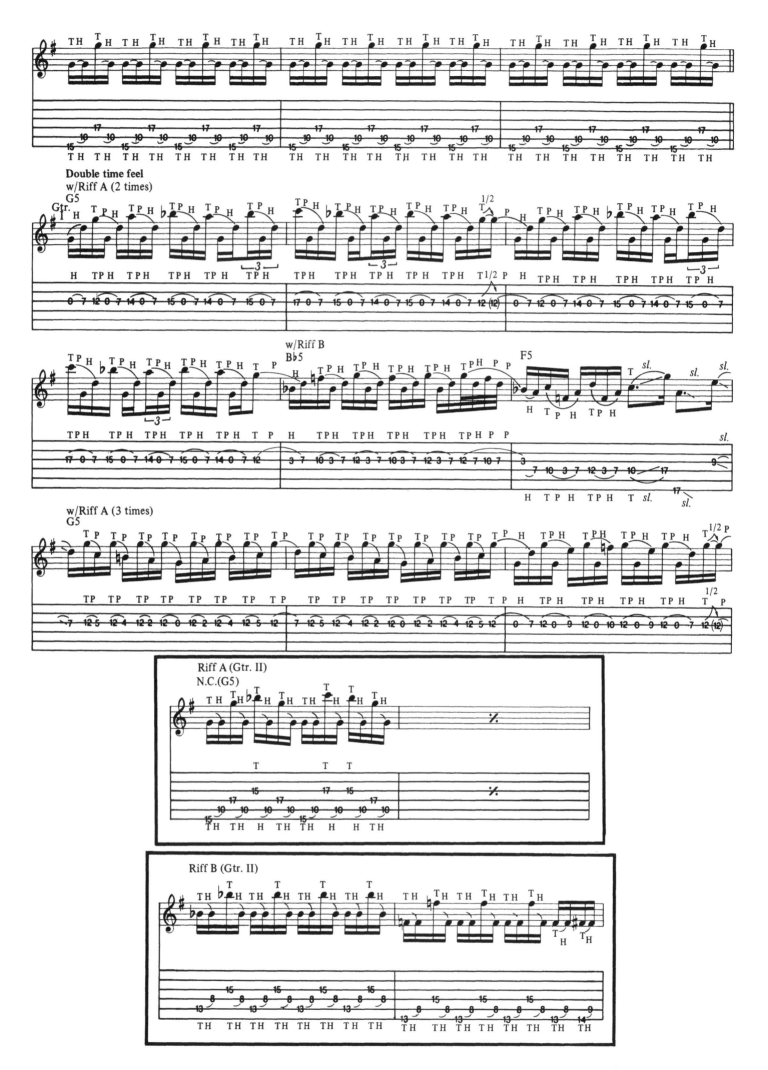

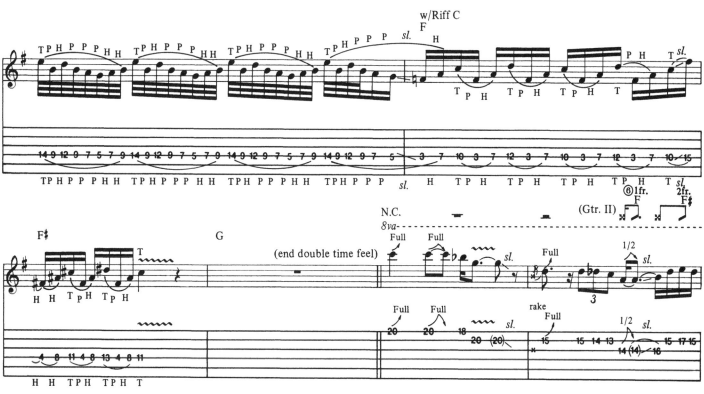

*Tap G w/r.h. middle finger and pull off to r.h. index finger.

from Testament - *Practice What You Preach*

PRACTICE WHAT YOU PREACH

Words and Music by
Eric Peterson, Luciano Clemente,
Alex Skolnick, Gregory Christian
and Charles Billy

A **Introduction**

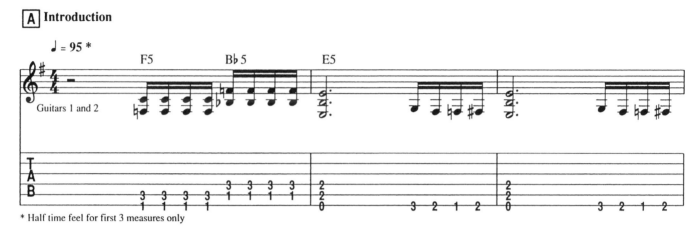

* Half time feel for first 3 measures only

* Double time feel throughout

B Verse

You _____ think your life's __ so grand, __ You don't be – lieve __ a word __ you say, __

Fig.1 variation

your _ feet aren't on ___ the ground _ you let __ your life just slip _ a – way. _

Guitars play Fig.1

Just _ so un – cer – tain of __ your bod – y and your soul. _

Guitars play Fig.1

The prom – is – es ___ you make, _ your mind _ goes blank _ and then you lose _ con – trol. _

Chorus

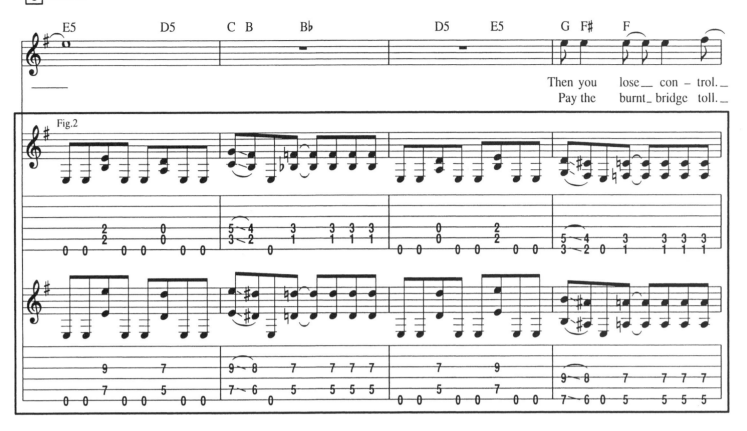

Then you   lose __ con - trol. __
Pay the   burnt_ bridge toll. __

Guitars play Fig.2

To Coda ⊕

(vocal second time only) Then   you lose __ con - trol._

Verse

Guitars play Fig.1 variation

I   nev – er   was __   the one, __   the one __   to   say __   the   things you say. __

Nev – er seem   to won – der __   what you say. __

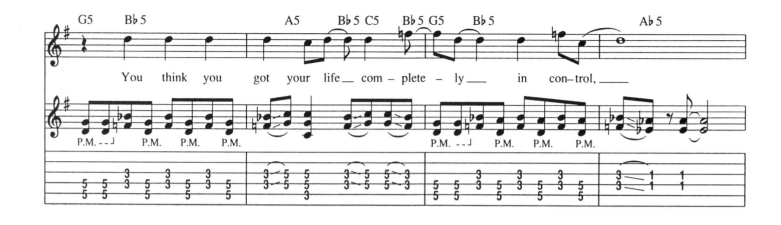

You think you got your life__ com – plete – ly __ in con–trol, ____

P.M. - - ⌐   P.M.   P.M.   P.M.   P.M. - - ⌐   P.M.   P.M.   P.M.

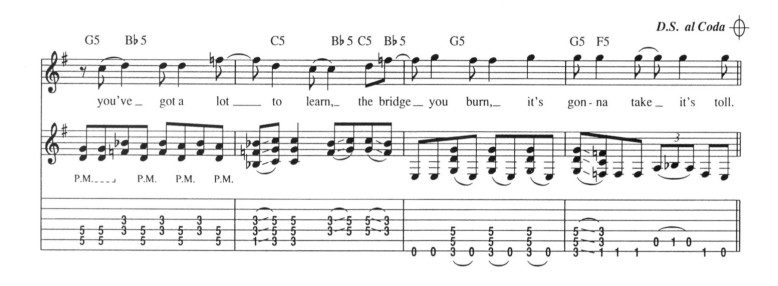

D.S. al Coda ✛

you've __ got a lot __ to learn,__ the bridge __ you burn,__ it's gon - na take _ it's toll.

P.M. - - ⌐   P.M.   P.M.   P.M.

✛ *Coda*

E Chorus

Guitars play Fig.2

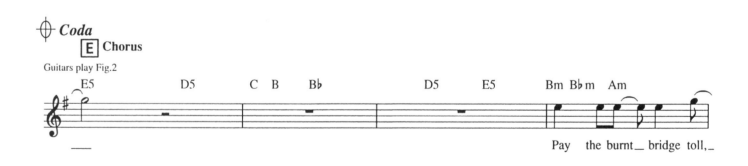

__   Pay the burnt __ bridge toll,__

Guitars play Fig.2

__   So prac – tice what _ you preach,__

104

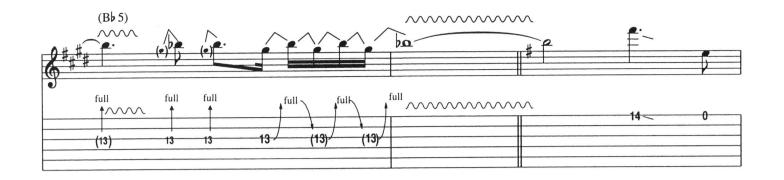

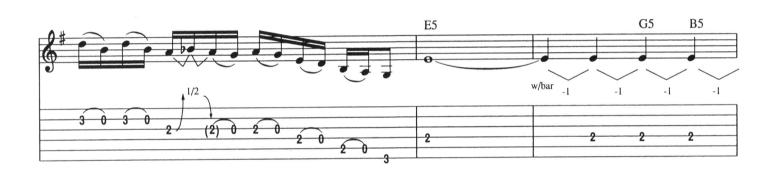

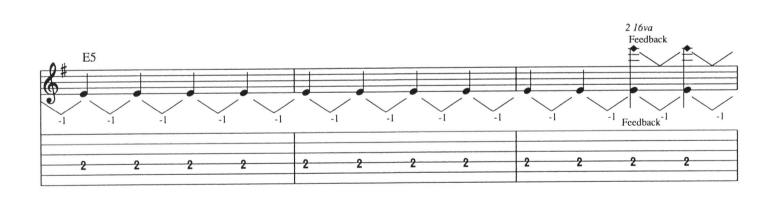

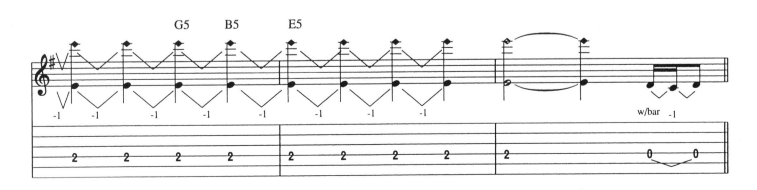

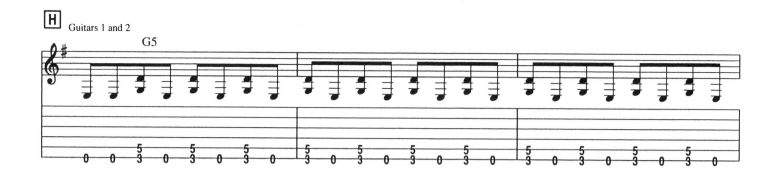

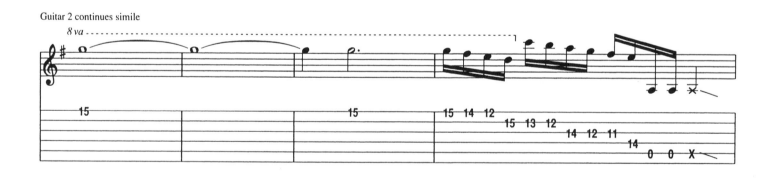

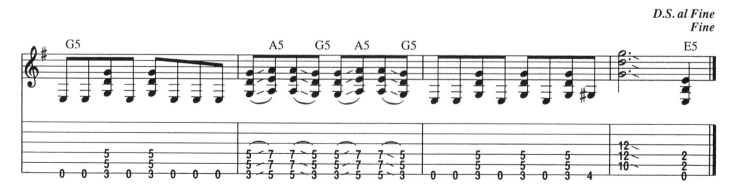

from Scorpions - *Taken by Force*

SAILS OF CHARON

Words and Music by Uli Roth

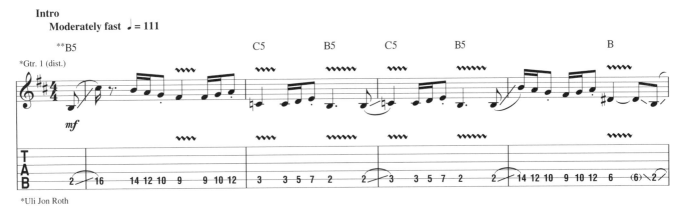

*Gtr. 1 (dist.)

mf

*Uli Jon Roth
**Chord symbols reflect implied harmony.

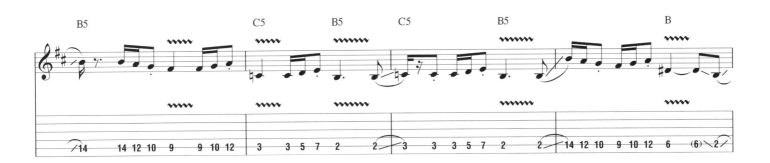

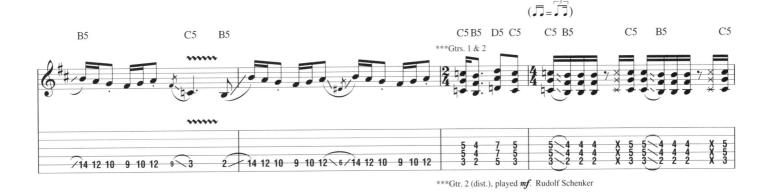

***Gtrs. 1 & 2

***Gtr. 2 (dist.), played *mf*. Rudolf Schenker

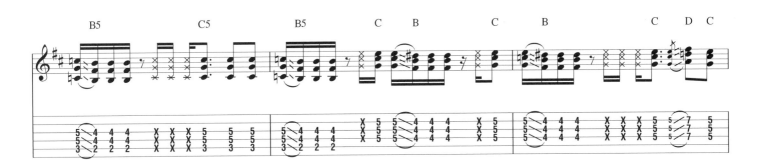

*Played as even sixteenth-notes.

119

from Black Label Society - *The Blessed Hellride*

STILLBORN

Written by Zachary Wylde

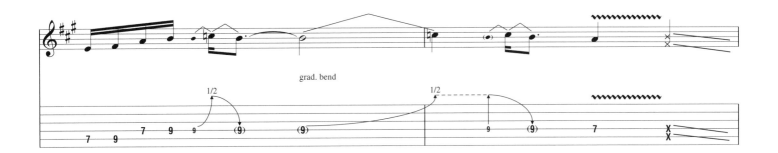

grad. bend

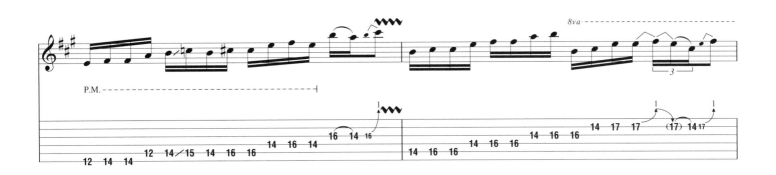

P.M.

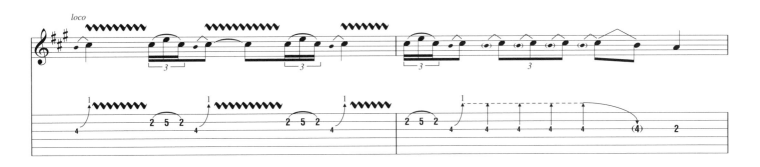

D.S. al Coda
(take 2nd ending)

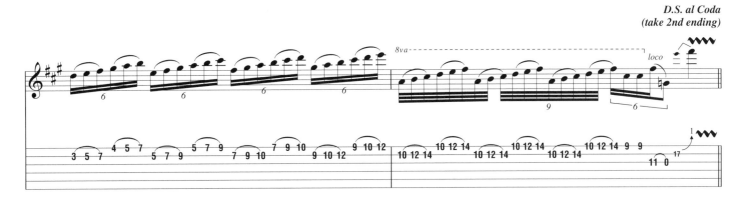

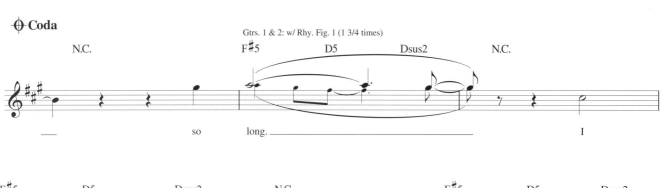

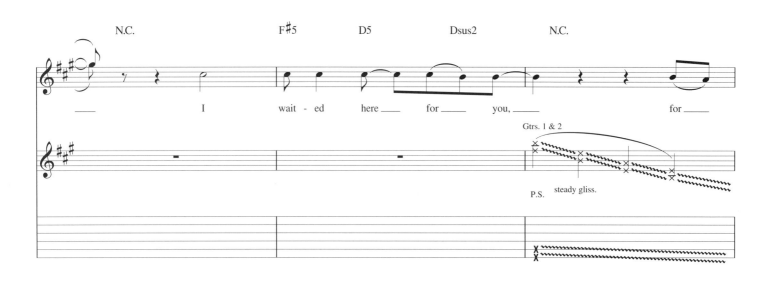

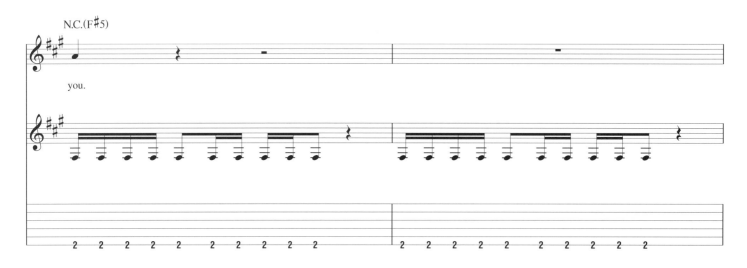

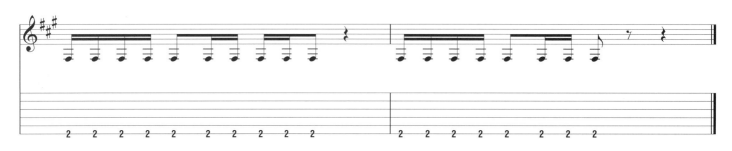

from Joe Satriani - *Surfing with the Alien*

SURFING WITH THE ALIEN

By Joe Satriani

126

*Pull up bar gradually.

**Depress bar before
striking note.

133

*Depress bar fully   †Tapped harmonic.
before striking note.   **Pull bar up.

from Dream Theater - *Images and Words*

TAKE THE TIME

Words and Music by
James LaBrie, Kevin Moore,
John Myung, John Petrucci
and Michael Portnoy

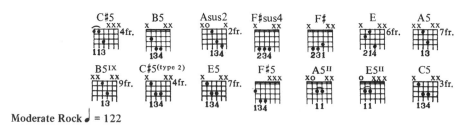

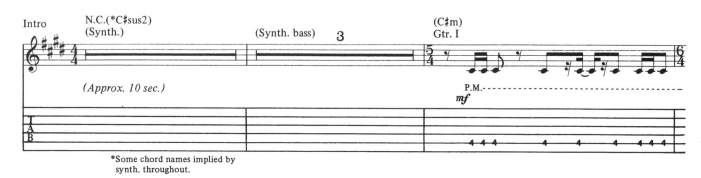

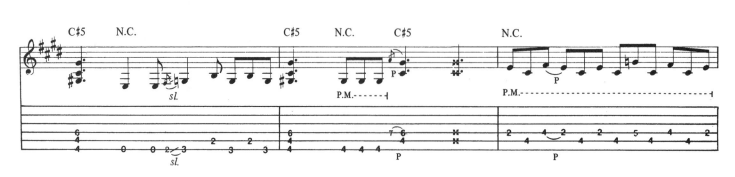

*Note is sustained through next bar
w/wide vibrato.

real.___ I feel the heat___ with-in___ my mind,___ and craft new chang-es___ with___ my

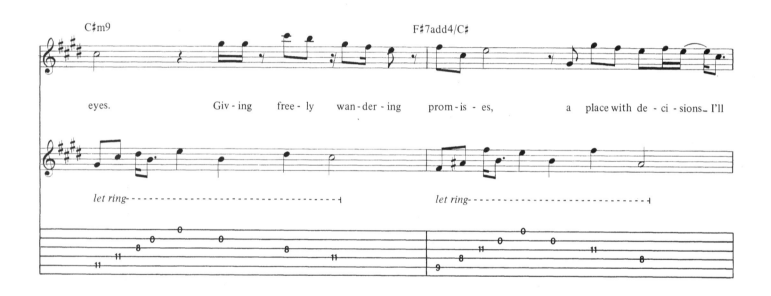

eyes. Giv-ing free-ly wan-der-ing prom-is-es, a place with de-ci-sions___ I'll

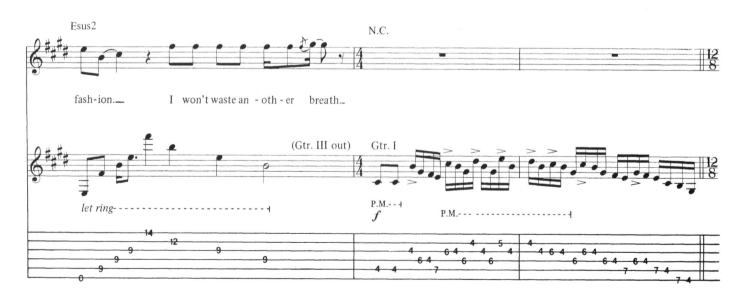

fash-ion.___ I won't waste an-oth-er breath.___

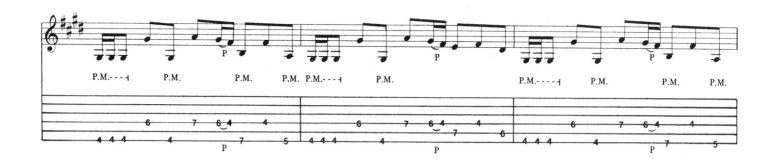

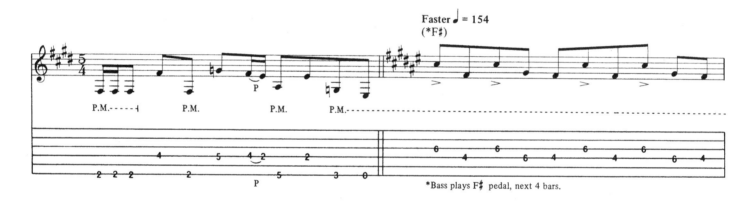

*Bass plays F♯ pedal, next 4 bars.

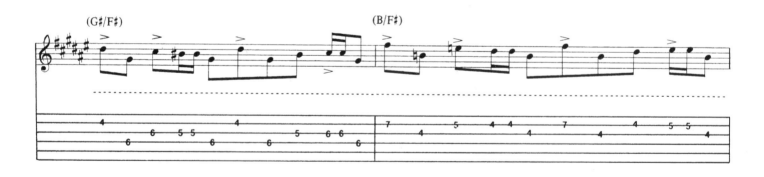

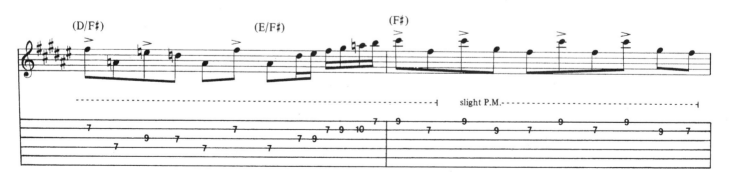

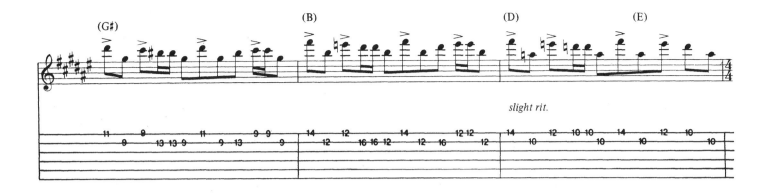

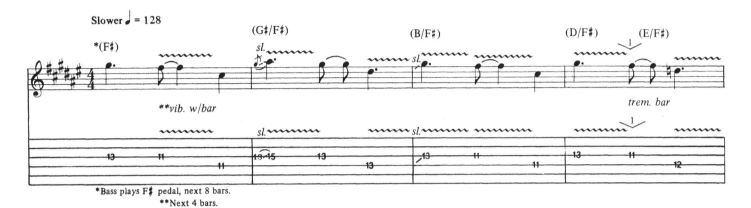

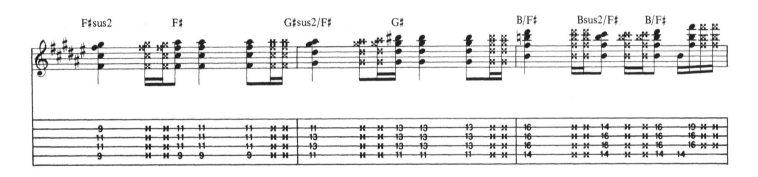

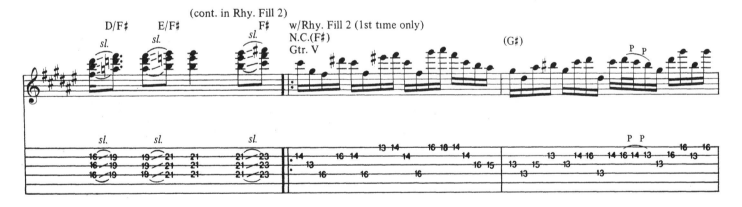

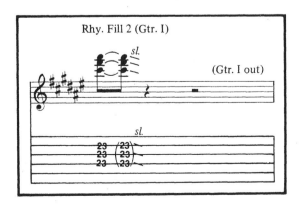

*Chord names implied
 by bass part.

A.H. pitch: D

A.H. pitch: G#

148

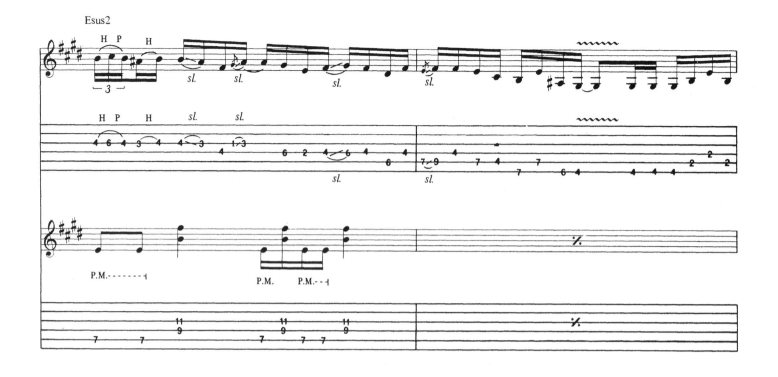

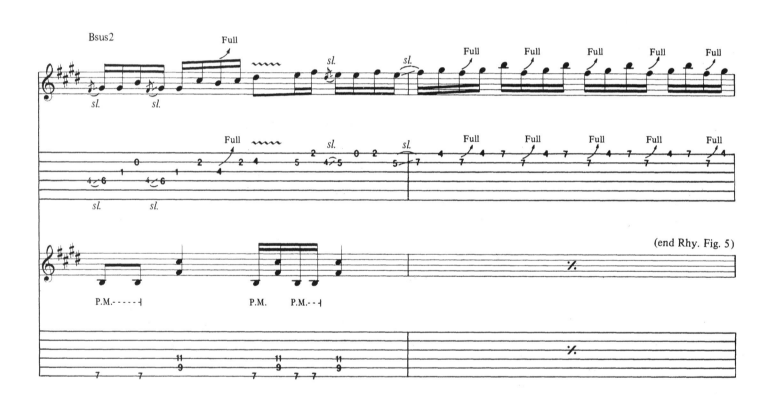

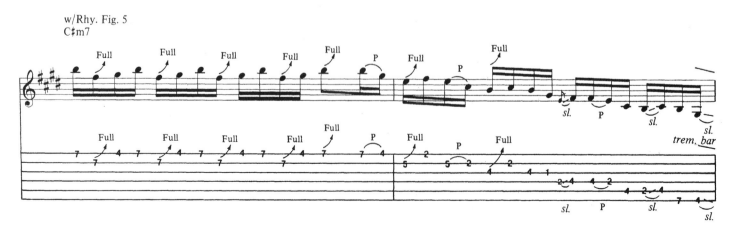

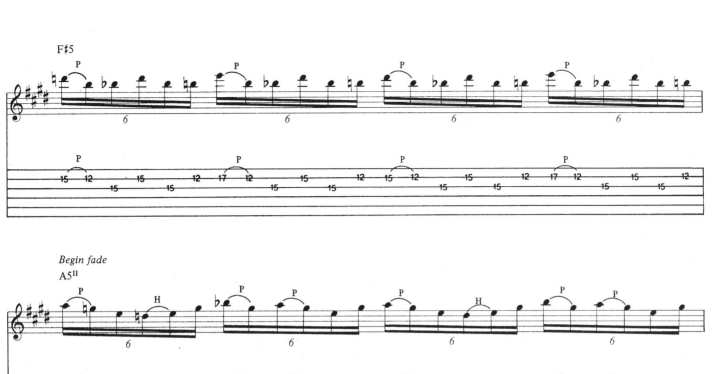

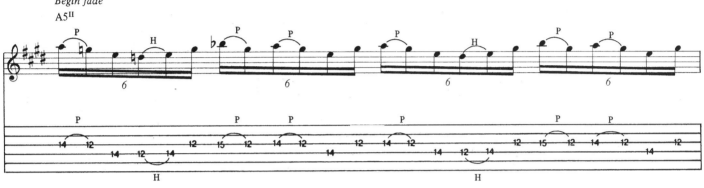

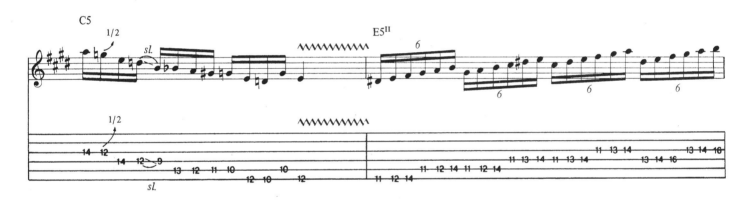

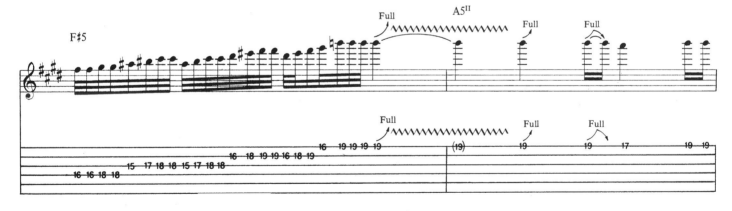

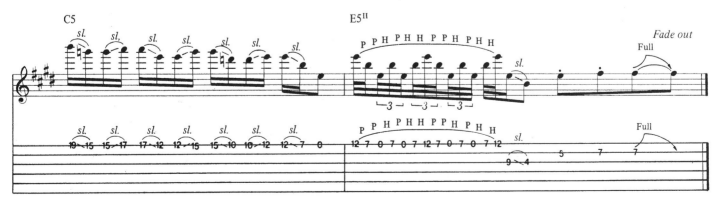

WHEN WILL I

Words and Music by
Monte Montgomery
and Scott Byers

Tune down 1/2 step:
(low to high) E♭-A♭-D♭-G♭-B♭-E♭

Intro
Moderately slow ♩ = 96

*A

Gtr. 1 (acous.)

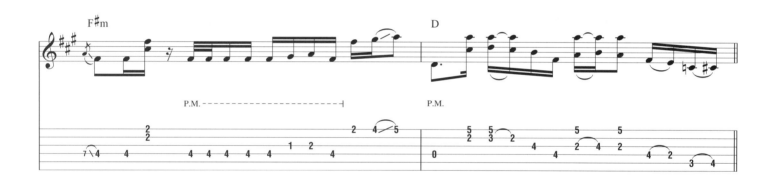

mf

w/ pick & fingers
let ring throughout

*Chord symbols reflect basic harmony.

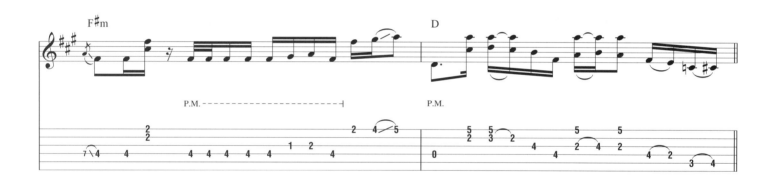

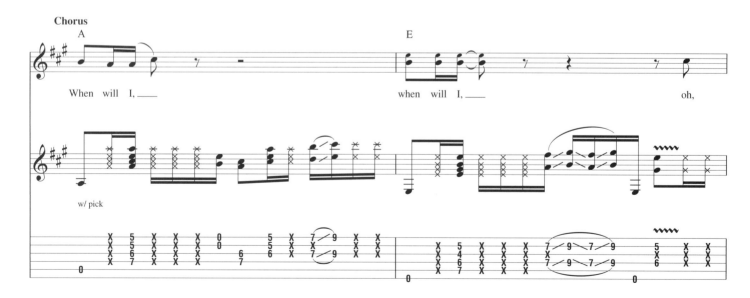

Chorus

A

When will I, _____

E

when will I, _____

oh,

w/ pick

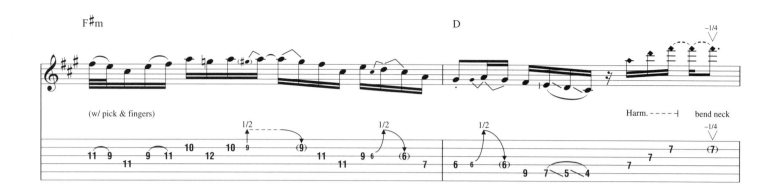

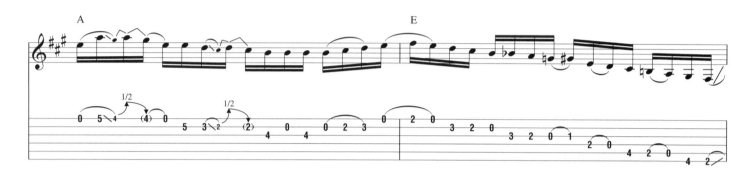

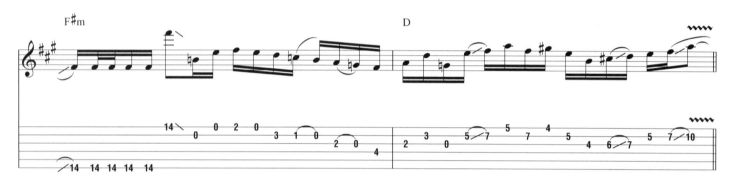

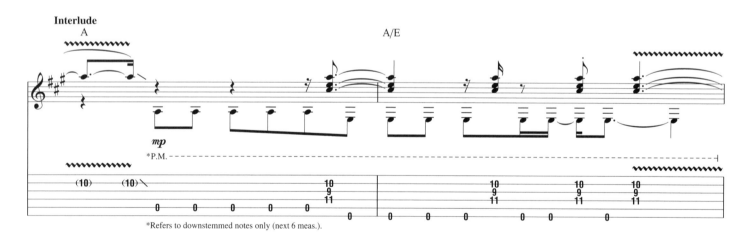

*Refers to downstemmed notes only (next 6 meas.).

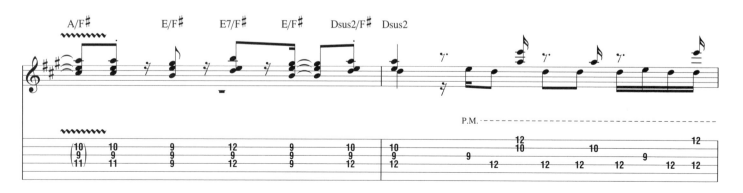

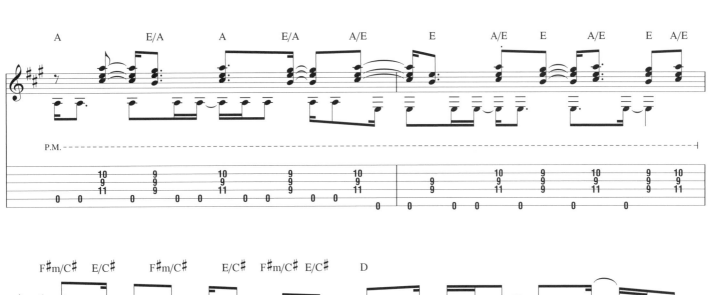

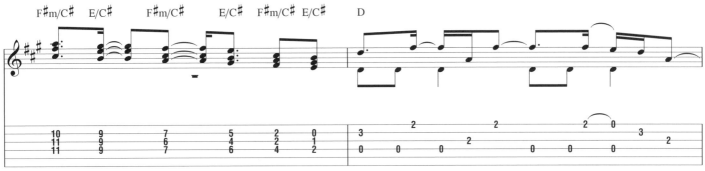

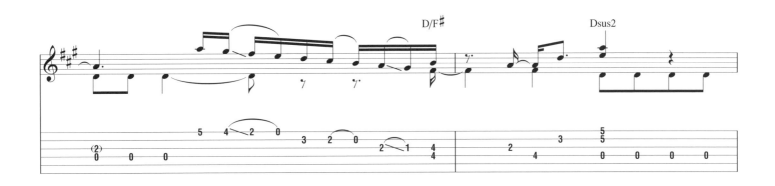

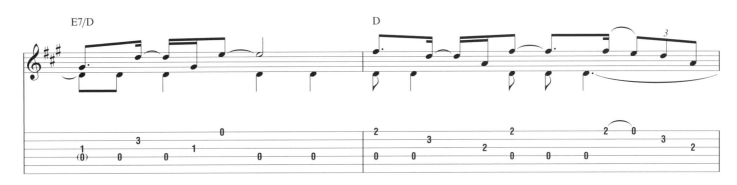

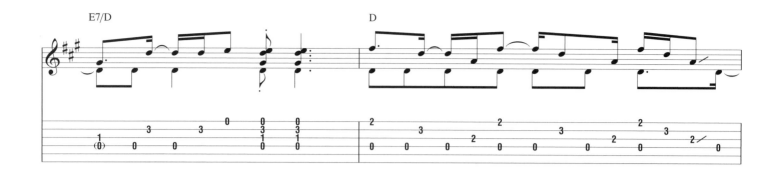

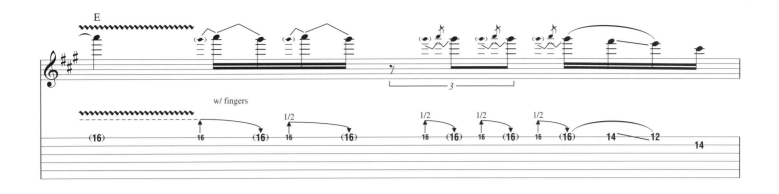

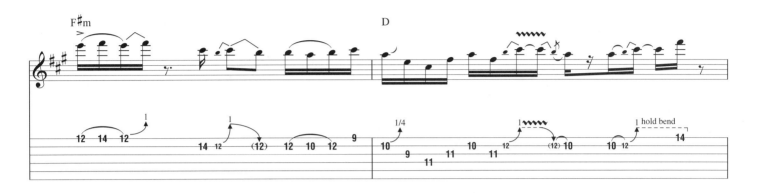

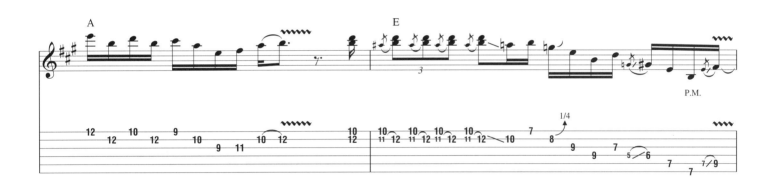

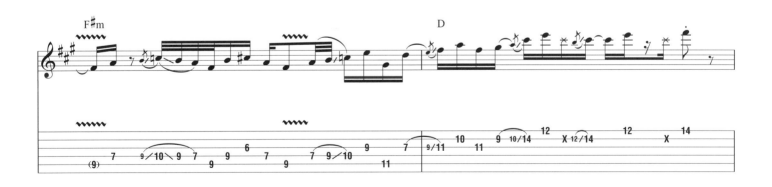

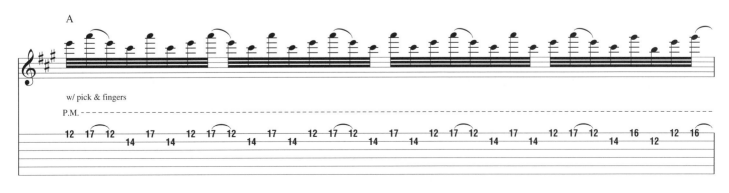

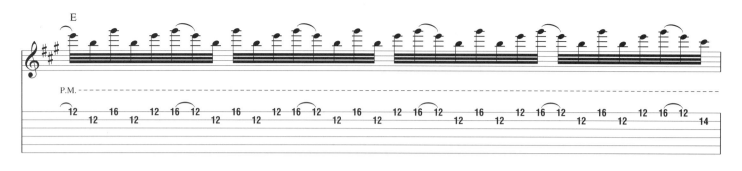

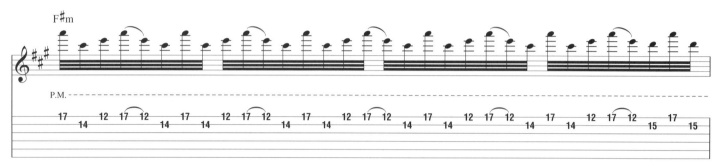

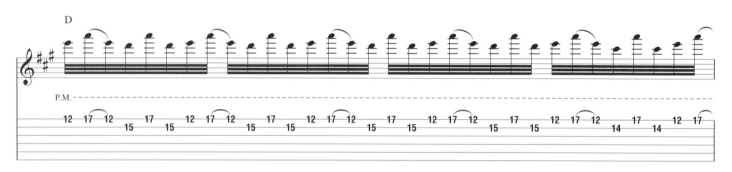

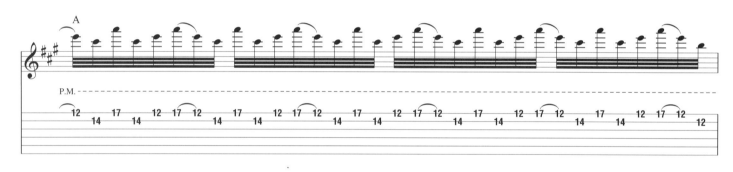

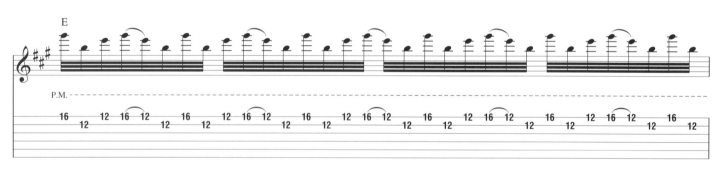

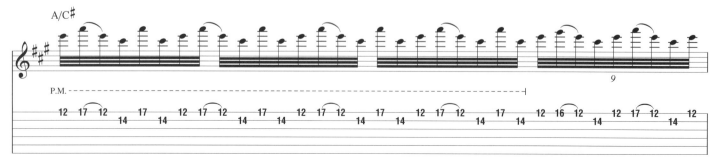

170

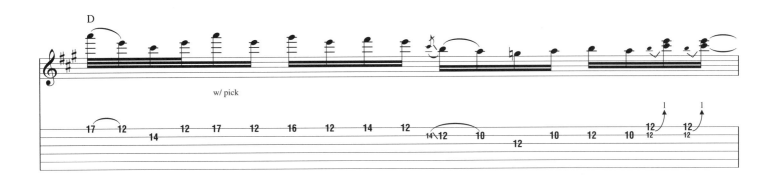

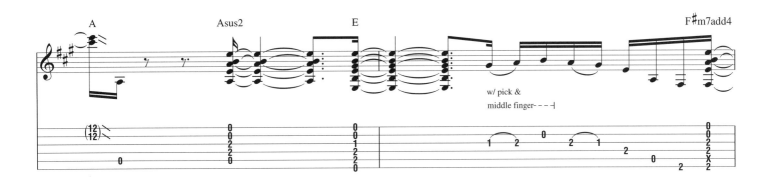

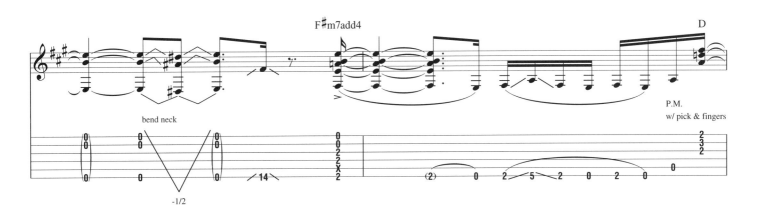

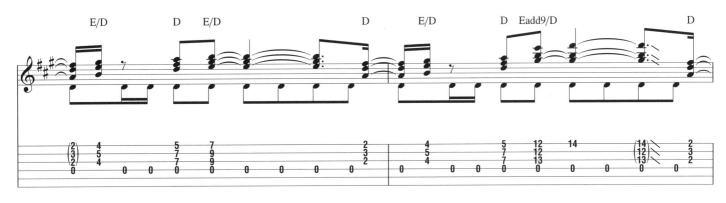

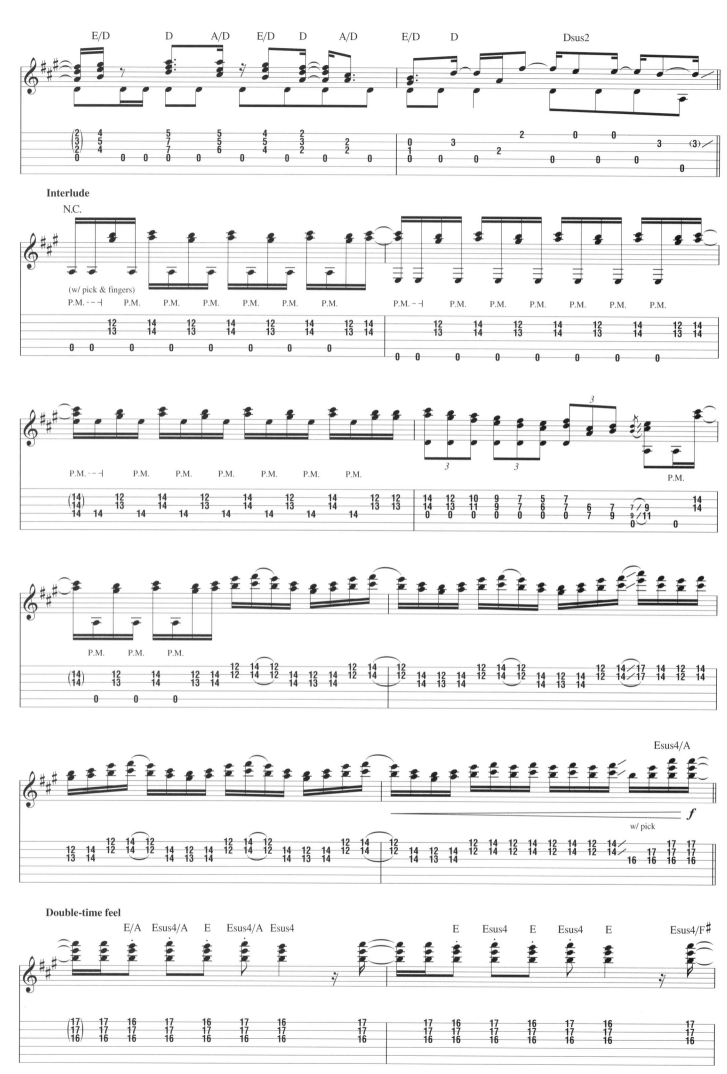

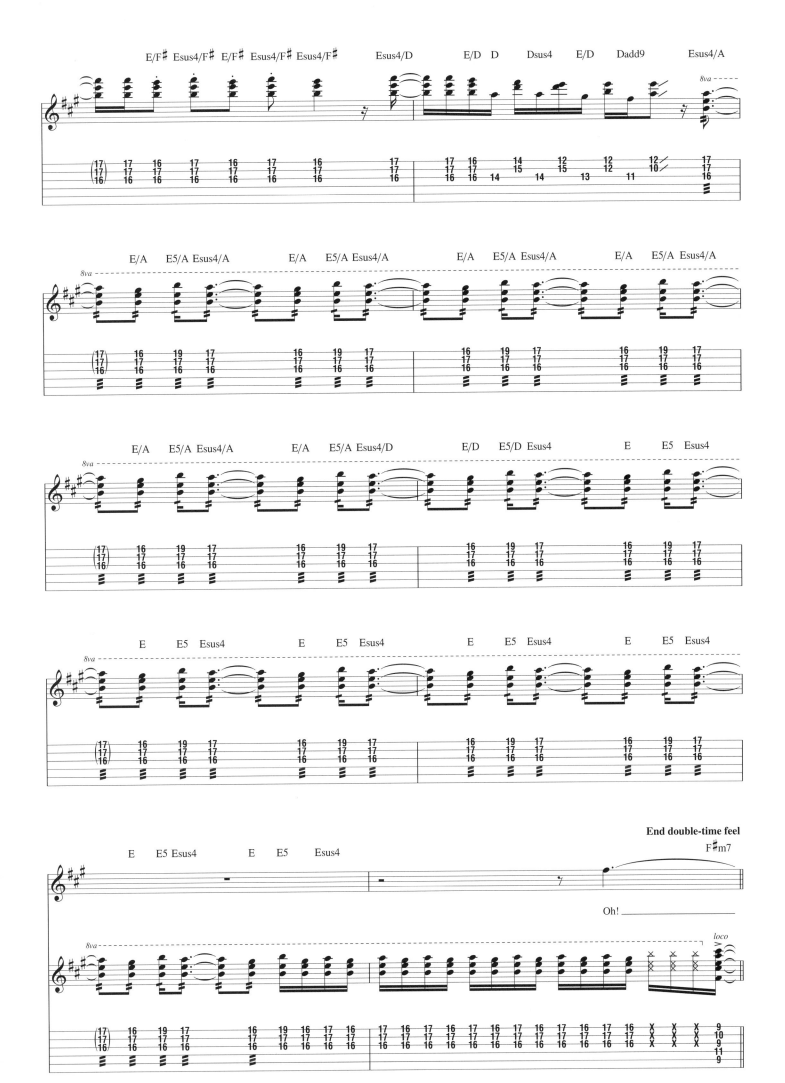

from Allan Holdsworth - *I.O.U.*

WHITE LINE

Words and Music by
Peter Brown and Allan Holdsworth

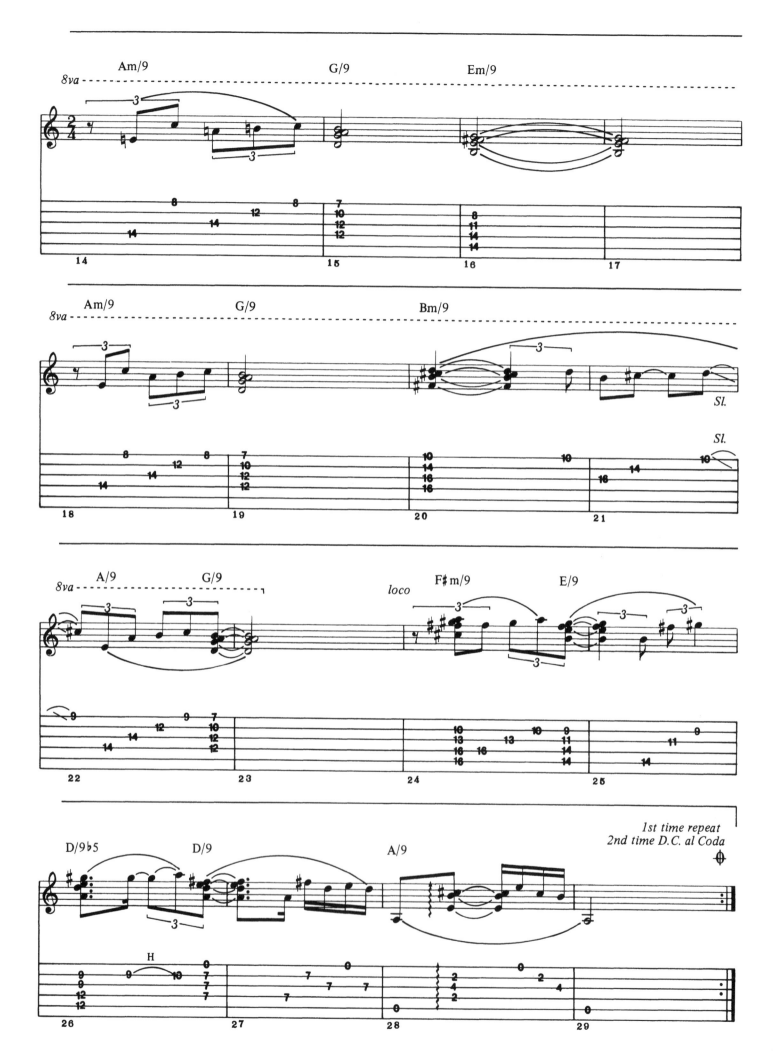

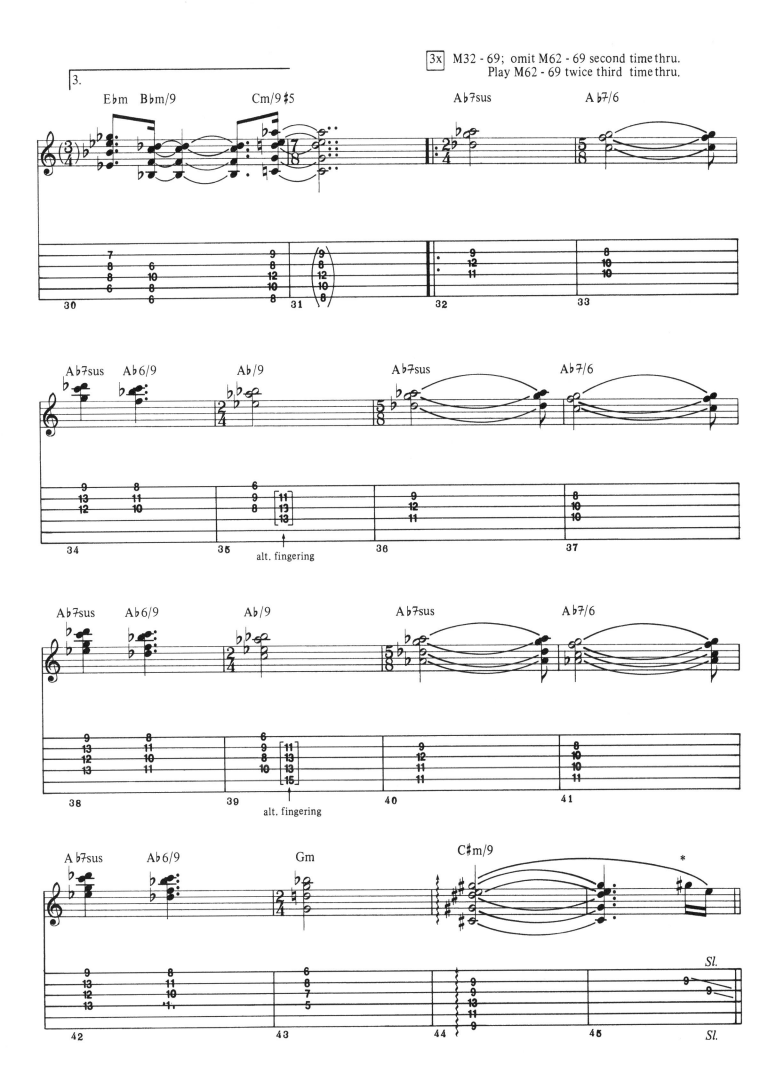

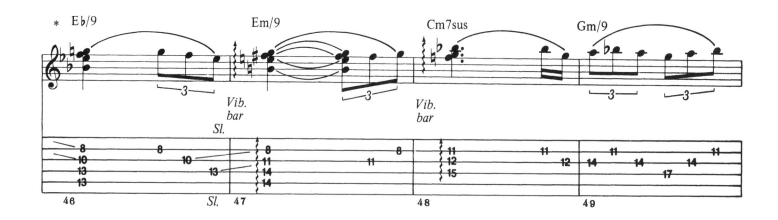

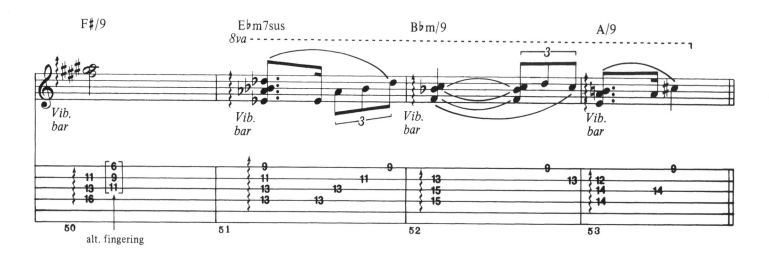

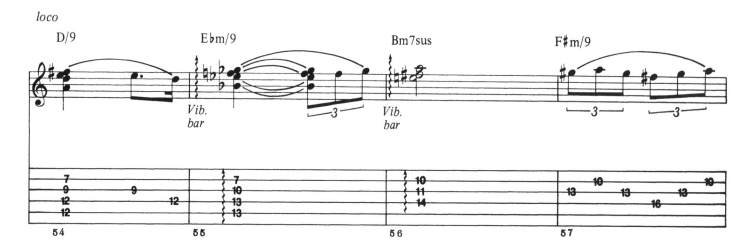

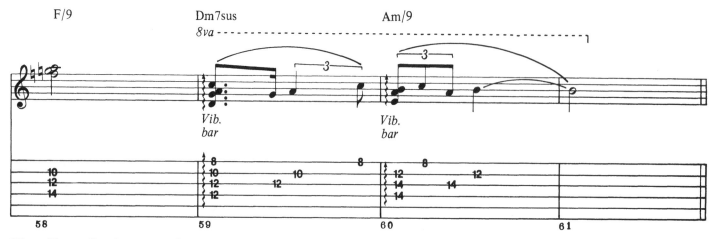

*See tablature line for correct slides and effects.

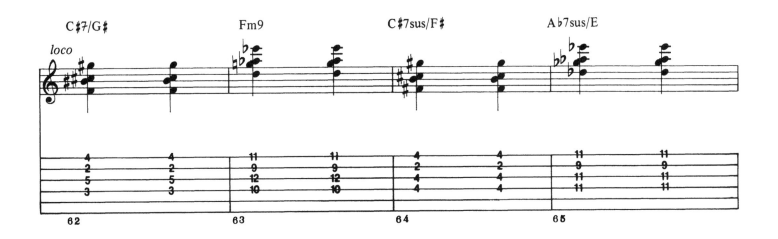

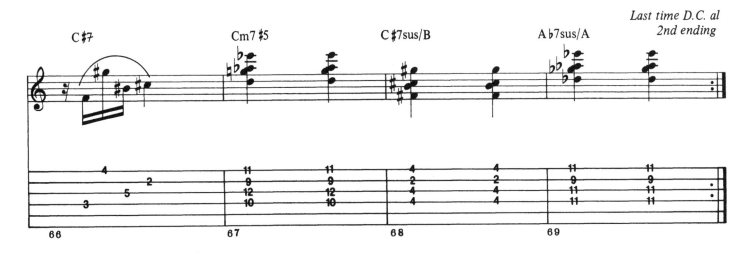

*Last time D.C. al
2nd ending*

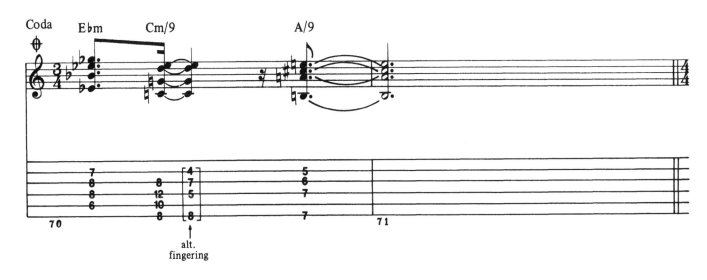

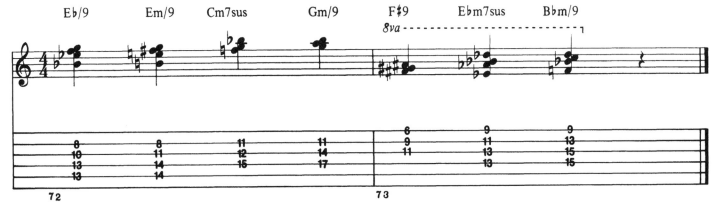

GUITAR NOTATION LEGEND

Guitar music can be notated three different ways: on a *musical staff*, in *tablature*, and in *rhythm slashes*.

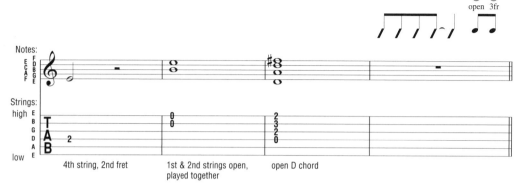

RHYTHM SLASHES are written above the staff. Strum chords in the rhythm indicated. Use the chord diagrams found at the top of the first page of the transcription for the appropriate chord voicings. Round noteheads indicate single notes.

THE MUSICAL STAFF shows pitches and rhythms and is divided by bar lines into measures. Pitches are named after the first seven letters of the alphabet.

TABLATURE graphically represents the guitar fingerboard. Each horizontal line represents a string, and each number represents a fret.

4th string, 2nd fret   1st & 2nd strings open, played together   open D chord

HALF-STEP BEND: Strike the note and bend up 1/2 step.

BEND AND RELEASE: Strike the note and bend up as indicated, then release back to the original note. Only the first note is struck.

HAMMER-ON: Strike the first (lower) note with one finger, then sound the higher note (on the same string) with another finger by fretting it without picking.

TRILL: Very rapidly alternate between the notes indicated by continuously hammering on and pulling off.

PICK SCRAPE: The edge of the pick is rubbed down (or up) the string, producing a scratchy sound.

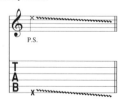

TREMOLO PICKING: The note is picked as rapidly and continuously as possible.

WHOLE-STEP BEND: Strike the note and bend up one step.

PRE-BEND: Bend the note as indicated, then strike it.

PULL-OFF: Place both fingers on the notes to be sounded. Strike the first note and without picking, pull the finger off to sound the second (lower) note.

TAPPING: Hammer ("tap") the fret indicated with the pick-hand index or middle finger and pull off to the note fretted by the fret hand.

MUFFLED STRINGS: A percussive sound is produced by laying the fret hand across the string(s) without depressing, and striking them with the pick hand.

VIBRATO BAR DIVE AND RETURN: The pitch of the note or chord is dropped a specified number of steps (in rhythm), then returned to the original pitch.

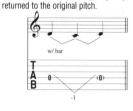

GRACE NOTE BEND: Strike the note and immediately bend up as indicated.

VIBRATO: The string is vibrated by rapidly bending and releasing the note with the fretting hand.

LEGATO SLIDE: Strike the first note and then slide the same fret-hand finger up or down to the second note. The second note is not struck.

NATURAL HARMONIC: Strike the note while the fret-hand lightly touches the string directly over the fret indicated.

PALM MUTING: The note is partially muted by the pick hand lightly touching the string(s) just before the bridge.

VIBRATO BAR SCOOP: Depress the bar just before striking the note, then quickly release the bar.

SLIGHT (MICROTONE) BEND: Strike the note and bend up 1/4 step.

WIDE VIBRATO: The pitch is varied to a greater degree by vibrating with the fretting hand.

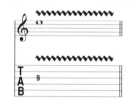

SHIFT SLIDE: Same as legato slide, except the second note is struck.

PINCH HARMONIC: The note is fretted normally and a harmonic is produced by adding the edge of the thumb or the tip of the index finger of the pick hand to the normal pick attack.

RAKE: Drag the pick across the strings indicated with a single motion.

VIBRATO BAR DIP: Strike the note and then immediately drop a specified number of steps, then release back to the original pitch.